A Creative Dictionary of Edwinstowe

Edited by
*Stephan Collishaw and
Liz Stewart-Smith*

Preface by
Alan Sillitoe

Edwinstowe Reading Group

A Creative Dictionary
of Edwinstowe

Published in 2005
by Edwinstowe Reading Group
c/o Edwinstowe Library,
High Street, Edwinstowe, Nottingham

ISBN 090712318X

Printed by Russell Press
Typeset and designed by 4 Sheets Design & Print Ltd.

**Nottinghamshire
County Council**
Community Services

Assisted by
THE
EUROPEAN
REGIONAL
DEVELOPMENT
FUND

Preface

We all know that one of the greatest regrets, after parents or relations have died, is not having talked to them enough about what they remembered of their past. Memories are common to everyone, but few think of recording them, unless verbally and within their own families. They might take them down onto a tape recorder, with the intention of committing them afterwards to paper, but if they then forget, the task is only half done.

Reminiscences of life gone by, in the form of reactions to historic events, and domestic data which is just as priceless, are kept alive for the benefit of the present but, rather more important, for the future as well. Those who come after us need some idea as to how people — we — existed in what will soon however become their past. Not only are we given the opportunity of comparing former social conditions with our own, we can also exercise our imaginations sufficiently to see them in some framework of reality.

That, of course, is not the sole purpose of this collection of verses, articles, and prose pieces, yet most of them do reinforce the point of the above remarks, to the extent that everything written forms some record of the past in showing how people lived. They also — and this is just as vital — tell us what they thought and how their minds worked. In this way is the value of the memorials enhanced.

I found this book stimulating to read, with something of interest on every page, and I feel sure that whoever takes it up will derive from it the same pleasure as myself.

Alan Sillitoe

Acknowledgements

Funding for this project was provided by Nottinghamshire County Council. Many thanks to Alan Sillitoe for his preface, and to Ross Bradshaw and Sara Hulse for their help. Thanks also to Edwinstowe library for hosting events and to the writers who have contributed articles: Greg Abbott, Sue Allen, Joseph Bennett, Pam Bird (extracts from *Growing up in a Mining Village*), Bill Currie, Gill Empson, Betty Ann Glover, Sara Hulse, Enid Johnson, Richard Nardini, Sheila Norton, Liz Stewart-Smith, Dennis Wood and Margaret Woodhead. Rimas Vainoras deserves thanks for his beautiful photographs. Thanks also to Margaret Woodhead for sharing her knowledge of the history of the village, and to Joseph Bennett, Pam Bird, Margaret Brocklehurst and Edwinstowe Historical Society for lending us photographs.

Sue Allen's poem *Heartless* was written for *Poets in Pink* and *Men are Like Bras* first appeared in *Angels in Asda*.

Introduction

Brewer's *Dictionary of Phrase and Fable* is not a dictionary. Nor does it deal solely with phrases and fables. It is hard to define precisely what the book is. It is easier to define the curious reader's reaction to it. Terry Pratchett compares it to a bag of peanuts: "Reading one item in Brewer's is like eating one peanut. It's practically impossible." Glancing into it as a teenager, I would occasionally find the word I was looking for, but more often than not I would be distracted along the way — waylaid by other words, introduced to arcane wisdom, knights and legends, to the Nunawading Messiah and other esoteric gems.

Within the first few pages of Brewer's dictionary the origin of Abracadabra is explained, we are introduced to the Semitic alphabet's curious shapes, to the 99 names of Allah. You look up from the text to find it has suddenly gone dark, your cup of tea is cold and the hour you set aside for your writing has been swallowed.

Brewer, born in 1810 in Norwich, spent the last years of his life in the little village of Edwinstowe. He died there in 1897 and is buried in the churchyard. His grave, shaded by a beech tree, is marked with a cross. You can read more about him in Liz Stewart-Smith's contribution under the letter U.

This project was developed to celebrate Brewer's connection to Edwinstowe. What you hold in your hands is, like Brewer's, hard to define, if more modest in scope and intention. In part it is an encyclopaedia of curious facts about Edwinstowe collated by Liz Stewart-Smith. It is also a collection of stories, poetry and memoir written by people living or working in Edwinstowe. Especially commissioned for the book are some beautiful photographs of the village by photographer Rimas Vainoras.

Pam Bird's account of growing up in the village of Edwinstowe — spread throughout the book — is a fascinating tale that mirrors the growth and changes that have taken place there since the early part of the twentieth century. There is of course a story about Robin Hood, though with a twist. There are also men, bras, sheep wardens, hooligans, nostalgia, eighteenth-century prisoners of war, ghosts, haiku, depression, Italians and old songs.

Like an encyclopaedia this book can be dipped into randomly. Like Brewer's perhaps also, once you start you will be caught and glance up and find the light has gone, the dinner hasn't been cooked and your cup of tea is cold. Certainly you'll learn that there is more to Edwinstowe than Robin Hood and Maid Marian.

Stephan Collishaw

ACORN

Started in May 1992 by Shirley Moore, with the help of a team of volunteers, this very successful community newspaper is published four times a year and delivered free to every house in the village. Although it relies on advertising revenue, every issue has a generous number of photographs, reminiscences of village life and articles about local events. Bound copies are kept in the Library. (For further details, contact: Shirley Moore 01623 822264.)

ARCHWAY HOUSE

Also known as Duke's Folly, Archway House is now a private residence. It was built as a hunting lodge in 1842 by the 5th Duke of Portland. He later used it as a school for 50 poor children. The carved figures on the upper storey of the building portray Robin Hood, Maid Marian, Little John, Richard I and Alan-a-Dale. The Duke wanted this copy of Worksop Priory gatehouse to be sited on a 21-mile avenue of trees between Welbeck Abbey and Nottingham.

A Short History of Edwinstowe Village

Edwinstowe (Edwin's place) is named after an early British Christian king called Edwin. He was converted to Christianity in AD 625 following persuasion by his wife Princess Ethelburga, who had come from Kent — the first Christian kingdom in England. Edwin was killed in AD 633 in a battle not too far from here. His followers buried him in a clearing in Sherwood Forest, intending to come back later to give him a proper king's burial. They put up a wooden chapel on the spot, as people were already visiting his grave and calling him St Edwin. The entry in the Domesday survey 400 years later suggests the church was still the only building. Subsequently, the village grew around the church, rather than the usual practice of a village growing and having a church built.

Sherwood Forest was designated a royal forest, which prevented even the taking of wood, let alone hunting for deer. It was easy to get into trouble and get outside the law (to become an outlaw!). Even the priest of St Mary's church was, in 1334, convicted of venison trespass — a serious offence. Although there is no record of what happened next it might be significant that a new priest was installed in 1335.

The land around was poor for agriculture so it must have been tempting to hunt for your food. Even visiting the forest today it is easy to imagine how a whole army could hide without detection, let alone a band of outlaws in the times of the Norman and Plantagenet kings.

As part of the penance of Henry II for the death of Beckett, the church of St Mary's was rebuilt in stone in 1175. This typical Norman church was extended in 1350 and in 1450, when the 46-metre spire was added. It collapsed, struck by lightning, in 1672. Only by writing to Charles II for permission to sell fallen oak trees from the royal forest could the villagers afford to rebuild it.

The next village, now called by its original name of

King's Clipstone (Old Clipstone on most maps) has a small ruin called King John's Palace. This is the site of the king's hunting 'lodge'. The palace was large — in 1281 Edward I had extra stables built for 200 more horses. In one king's visit of 1315, 100 pike and 1,600 roach were taken from fishponds to feed the guests.

For over 200 years, all the kings of England regularly visited and stayed here. Even Richard the Lionheart, who was only in England for eight months of his nine-year reign, visited twice.

The village of Edwinstowe has remained quite small for most of its existence. In the late seventeenth century the lands of the royal forest began to be sold off by the crown, notably to the soon-to-be Duke of Newcastle and the Duke of Portland. The large estates in the vicinity have given the area its general name — the Dukeries.

Edwinstowe grew slowly, as it was still difficult to travel to the area. Most people worked on the local estates and the Manvers estate (Thoresby) owned much of the village until the 1940s.

However, all was not well. In 1833 the Oddfellows Lodge was formed to educate the village inhabitants and draw them away from lawless drunken behaviour. Attempts were made to turn "gross lumps of ignorance into Christian men".

The village constable for many years was a former Bow Street officer. Henry James Perrener lived in the constable's cottage (now Robin's Pantry) before his death in 1841. He is buried in St Mary's churchyard. The original village lock-up is still in the backyard of the cottage.

The railway reached Edwinstowe in 1893, with the first train from nearby Mansfield running in 1899. This allowed a large increase in visitors. In 1912, Mrs Emiline Pankhurst and her suffragettes visited. It is said 20 of them went inside the Major Oak, setting a new record.

The major expansion of Edwinstowe village was in 1925, when nearly 500 houses were built to serve the new coal mine. This is still in operation, under its original name of Thoresby Colliery.

The 1960s saw more houses being built, as people's desire to live in the countryside increased and was made easier thanks to the growth in ownership of the family car. New dwellings are still being added each year.

Sherwood Forest is a site of international importance for flora and fauna. It now receives visitors from all over the world throughout the year. Many are attracted by the legend of Robin Hood and his marriage in St Mary's church to Lady Marian — it is the stuff of Hollywood. However, written evidence of the time is sparse and, as only the rich and important wrote the history books, outlaws have to remain mainly legend.

Greg Abbott

BAND — THORESBY COLLIERY BAND

In 1948, Welbeck Pit Band had been disbanded, and so was no longer able to accompany the Armistice Parade in Edwinstowe. The colliery manager, embarrassed at having to lead the procession from the Welfare Hall accompanied by a gramophone, arranged for Welbeck's instruments to be purchased for a new colliery band at Thoresby. Stan Lippeatt conducted the band for 17 years until January 2004. The band has competed successfully in national competitions, including winning Section One Brass Band Finals at the Royal Albert Hall in 2000. Dame Judi Dench is their Honorary Life Vice-President.

BOY BISHOP

At St Mary's Church the medieval custom of "Chylde Bishop" (from Salisbury Cathedral) was revived in the 1960s by Reverend Harold Pickles. On St Nicholas Day (6th December), a boy chorister of good character was elected to serve for a year — his duties included preaching a sermon and attending church every Sunday. In the 1980s, girls were also elected.

BREWER

After a successful career as schoolmaster and author, Reverend Dr Ebenezer Cobham Brewer moved into Edwinstowe Vicarage in 1884. He published more than 30 self-help books on subjects ranging from science to book-keeping. Although he was busy revising his *Dictionary of Phrase and Fable,* he gave a lecture about Darwin to a large audience at Ollerton Christian Association in December 1888, entitled "Is Man a Developed Monkey?" He conducted services, preached and took a lively interest in his grandchildren. He awarded an annual prize for the boys' mapping class in the village school. Brewer died in March 1897, aged 86, and is buried in Edwinstowe church-yard.

(**SEE ALSO:** COBHAM BREWER'S LABOUR OF LOVE BY LIZ STEWART-SMITH ON PAGE 107)

Growing up in a Mining Village in the 1930s and 1940s

1. Father

We marched shoulder to shoulder, banners unfurled, encouraged by tooting taxi drivers and enthusiastic whistles and shouts from well-wishers as they went about their business in the City.

What had driven me, a retired NHS Personnel Officer and an elected Councillor for a small village in Sherwood Forest, to march for the cause of the miners' right to work?

Miners, their families and friends were all here pounding the unfamiliar streets of Dick Whittington's city — their goal the elite establishment of the Houses of Parliament and the ears of the mighty parliamentarians.

The resolution of the marchers was strong and unwavering. As we marched behind the Collieries' brass bands, the miners told hilarious tales of their work, making light of their daily fear as they dropped in the cage to the very bowels of the earth. Humour was a gift from God, given to the miners to support them in their daily underground torment. As a daughter and granddaughter of a mining family, I was deeply moved. I needed to tell of the great moves forward that the mining fraternity had achieved in the twentieth century. The book, held captive so long in my head, was urging me to pen and paper. Childhood memories to be captured before miners were forgotten.

This is the story of a newly established mining village, its families and children. The family referred to is my own, but the trials, tribulations and subsequent high spots could equally well apply to any family that moved into the new coalfield villages of Nottinghamshire in the second quarter of the twentieth century.

The sequence of events is not written in chronological order. They have been written in the naive manner in which they occurred to me.

Most of us had been born in Edwinstowe, or had been brought there in infancy. No one had told us that we were poor and deprived children. We had no idea that to be a miner's child marked you down as very low in the social scale.

The typical miner of the flat cap, white muffler, whippets, racing pigeons and 'pit' language was very scarce, even non-existent in Edwinstowe.

The miners and their families travelled from collieries far and wide to live in this newly established mining village in the Robin Hood country of Sherwood Forest. All of them were looking for work and a settled life, allowing them to raise their families in a decent and stable environment.

These were hard and difficult times for all working-class people, none more so than the lot of the miner. Many of them were penniless but proud, hardworking and resilient people, life's bitter blows having taught them numerous lessons in survival.

They came from the worked out and abandoned pits of Yorkshire, County Durham, Derbyshire, Shropshire, Newcastle, Wales, Scotland and many other areas of the British Isles where miners had fallen on hard times.

My own family originated from beautiful Shropshire, but nowhere seems beautiful when you are destitute, out of work and with two growing daughters to feed.

At the youthful and innocent age of 17, my father Henry, along with many other jobless men, took the King's Shilling, marching out en masse from their village wearing the colours of the King's Shropshire Light Infantry to help win the war to end all wars.

Henry was just one of the very few who returned to his village in 1919, but not before he was severely wounded twice.

He came home from war a scarred, lice-ridden, bitter and disconsolate old man of 23 short years. He had seen many of his school friends and cousins die in the muddy, verminous trenches of France. Although a 'new world' had been promised for the victorious heroes, they were empty promises soon forgotten by mighty politicians.

He had endured a dreadful war of which he rarely spoke until his later years. He returned to a life of grinding poverty as a coal miner.

He became a disillusioned man in the strike of 1926, when miners' children were freezing and starving in rags on the streets, and politicians turned a blind eye to their fate. After many weeks of frustrated resentment on both sides the strike eventually came to a bitter end.

My father then made the momentous decision to move his family to look for a better life in the verdant land of Nottinghamshire, where rich seams of coal lay waiting to be plundered beneath Sherwood Forest and Robin Hood had reputedly robbed the rich to feed the poor.

The men came to the new collieries using any means of transport available at the time — walking for miles, hitching lifts from the carriers and in my dad's case cycling the 90-plus miles from Shropshire on an old and decrepit bicycle, the saddle of which had long since disintegrated and was now padded with an old sack. The brakes were non-existent, so my dad just pushed his feet into the spokes to grind to a halt when the necessity arose. On his back he carried his old army kitbag, which my mam had filled with as many provisions as she could spare from her meagre pantry.

His own mother, tearful at his departure again after the long and wearisome parting of the Great War years, contributed bread, cheese and beer, staples of all miners, and off he went to seek his fortune as Dick Whittington had done before him.

He was not to see his mother, father, brothers and sisters and his beloved Wrekin countryside for six long years — there was no money available to spare for luxuries like travelling to visit your distant relatives.

I have often wondered of his thoughts as he pedalled laboriously towards a new life. He had no promise of a job at the other end, just a belief in his own ability and desperate needs for his family.

13

On the way he stayed to rest in barns, ditches and hedgerows, in fact anywhere he could lay his weary head.

Many years later, during the war, when all road signs had been removed in case of invasion and in order to confuse the enemy, my sister Lucy and husband Arnold were embarking on an epic adventure. Having travelled many times to Shropshire by train, they were now going to pedal their tandem on the many miles to visit scattered relatives in Shropshire. They sought directions from dad — who had already cycled the route, albeit the other way.

He certainly gave them clear and concise instructions, listing all the names and locations of the pubs en route. It would seem his weary journey all those years ago had been liberally oiled by the hops and malt supped in these friendly hostelries.

My father remained homesick for his beloved Shropshire for most of his life, and his aim and ambition was always to return there on retirement. This was never an option, because by the time he was 65 he had formed his own dynasty of Nottinghamshire-born children and grandchildren, all of them settled in homes and work in the area. His immediate family ties were the stronger, and so he remained in Edwinstowe, where his ashes were eventually laid to rest beside his late wife, my mam Rose, in St Mary's churchyard.

The Bolsover Colliery Company had, after much negotiating, acquired land from the Earl of Manvers to sink Thoresby Colliery, a pit that was destined to become the jewel in the crown of modern mining in Great Britain. This was the pit in which my dad spent the remainder of his working days.

One of the greatest assets was that the pit was sunk well away from the village, consequently the residents were able to enjoy a relatively clean and healthy environment, although the miners' homes belched out smoke from their fireside grates all day long. Nevertheless the noise, fumes and smoke from the pit did not impinge upon the village life of Edwinstowe — a great plus to the miners returning

14

home after a gruelling shift in the depths of the earth.

After his long, lonely trek from Shropshire, my father arrived at Thoresby Colliery only to be told there was work, but not on a regular basis, and he would have to wait for the next tranche of houses to be built in Edwinstowe. He was therefore offered lodgings in a miner's home in New Ollerton.

He gladly accepted both conditions and began his daily queuing at the pitheads for work. Sometimes he was successful and other days he cycled back dejected on his boneshaker to his lodgings. Nevertheless that was it! He was established. Although only working one or two shifts a week he was able to send a pittance back home to his family in Shropshire.

The men, once established, sent for their unhappy wives, who were obviously reluctant to leave the historically close-knit communities of their birth, to come to live with strangers in a distant and unknown county. They were going to miss the warm clasp of their mother's arms, their school friends and familiar streets. They had no choice, their men had found work and it was their loving duty to follow them.

The amazing fact was that most of them became true Edwinstowians in a very short time, helping to lay the first foundations of the village as we know it today. A vibrant, pleasant and thriving community, proud of its forest and farming heritage, the mining tradition, and the evergreen legend of Robin Hood and his Merry Men.

Of course many of the miners went to work elsewhere in the Nottinghamshire coalfield, where similar villages had sprung up around the newly sunk pits — Clipstone, Bilsthorpe and New Ollerton to name but a few.

Edwinstowe had been, until the 1920s, a tiny rural village with very few amenities, inhabited mostly by farm workers and woodsmen who were employed on the Thoresby Estate.

Many of the villagers were horrified when they learnt of the plan to build several hundred houses for these

15

unknown, itinerant miners from distant parts.

The tiny village was to change forever. The new estate more than trebled the community in one fell swoop. However there is no doubt that some benefits were felt. For the first time an electricity supply was brought in, and muddy roads were metalled and lit. Mains sewerage was now available, surely an absolute luxury after the use of earth closets at the bottom of the gardens.

In the fullness of time my parents, two daughters and now a baby son were reunited and moved into their brand new house in 1928. They were to remain in this house until the sad and premature death of my mother at the age of 60 in 1956. The lively spirit of my mam had been extinguished: the house was no longer filled with her Shropshire tales and wit. The hum of the wireless, her constant companion from dawn to dusk, was hushed.

The family was devastated. My dad took his sorrow into a bungalow quite near to my home. Life had once again changed forever. Sad times.

However, when they first moved their scant possessions into their new home, they had for the first time in their lives a water closet, and hot and cold water ran lavishly in the kitchen and modern bathroom. They splashed happily in the bath, the children flushing the lavatory countless times a day. What luxury after lugging a tin bath in from the backyard every week. They also boasted 'The Room', which was kept for Sunday use only! Three bedrooms, a pantry and coalhouse completed the little palace. The whole house was radiant with electric light and coal fires danced in all the living quarters, but more importantly there was food in the larder and shoes on the children's feet. Surely the King himself could not have expected more.

To the front and rear there were large gardens and an entrance gate, shared only with next-door neighbours.

The gardens became the province of the menfolk, who were to be seen diligently planting, hoeing and weeding as they cultivated vegetables for their spartan table. They breathed in the fresh and bracing forest air as they grew colourful flowers in their front gardens: sweet peas, chrysanthemums and Michaelmas daisies wove a bewitching tapestry along the neat roads, but rarely did they allow them to be gathered and taken indoors. They knew too well what it was like to be incarcerated without a breath of God's fresh air on their cheeks. A far cry from the long rows of grimy cottages and backyards previously occupied in those distant mining villages. My parents must have thought they were in paradise, after their shabby little cottage in Madeley.

Did my mam and dad ever dream of the better times they now began experiencing? Times were still hard, money was short but life had at last begun to show a more promising outlook as they worked to clothe and feed us.

Pam Bird

CHARCOAL BURNING

Before coal was mined, forges at Carburton and Clipstone were totally reliant for their fuel on charcoal burners. Working alongside the woodcutters in Sherwood Forest, charcoal burners used timber that was unsuitable for building ships or houses.

Charcoal was produced by burning wood at a slow and controlled rate so that combustion was never complete. A mound of earth (called a clamp) was built and very little air was allowed to get in. After 24 hours 3–4 tons of timber would yield about 1 ton of charcoal.

CO-OP

Edwinstowe Co-op opened at the bottom of Town Street (High Street) in April 1895 with a loan from Earl Manvers of £250. Its aims were to promote thrift amongst his workers and to give them the "opportunity of buying not only some of the first necessities of life, but also other articles which at present are not procurable in the village, of good quality and upon fair terms". Members received tokens showing how much they had spent and full dividend on purchases made.

In 1894 there were 255 members, but by 1913 membership had fallen to 178. To ensure its survival, Edwinstowe Co-op had to amalgamate with Mansfield Co-op.

Edwinstowe Co-op, High Street, c1905. Mrs Wilfred Emerson, Henry Holmes (Butcher), George Smith (Co-op Carter) with his horse, Rocker.

CRICKETERS

An 1880 photograph shows the North Forest and Edwinstowe teams, which included the famous bowler, **Henry Morley**.

Alan Revill (1923–1998) grew up in the village and went on to play for Derbyshire, Leicestershire and Berkshire.

The Mating Game

A trip to town to buy the latest fashion creation. Hair in rollers while the make-up was carefully applied and the final touch of perfume — *Evening in Paris* or *Phul Nana*. The anticipation of getting ready for the dance while watching *Oh Boy* on TV.

"What are you wearing tonight?"

Might be a pencil skirt with a slit up, or the dress with all the petticoats that swirl out and reveal stocking tops and suspenders, when jiving to the rock and roll numbers the Pem Darch orchestra played so well. Stiletto shoes, of course, were the foot fashion item of the day.

The Edwinstowe Village Dance was **the** meeting place in the 1950s. Teenagers from all the surrounding villages met to enjoy themselves. They were from Forest Town, Clipstone, Worksop, Warsop, Mansfield Woodhouse, Wellow, and Ollerton. The bus service then was reliable and frequent and there was always 'late transport' supplied by Morley's Buses to transport us all back to our home village.

The girls would be there early, practising their body movements (no need for aerobics then). The lads would be in one of the local pubs having a drink, but they had to be at the dance by 10.00 or they were refused entry. No alcohol was supplied at the dance.

The Teddy boys were in their smart drainpipe-trousered suits and crepe-soled shoes. Some of them were still doing their National Service and anxious to let their hair down for the weekend — hair fashioned in the DA (duck's arse) style.

The various gangs used to congregate together and everyone wondered who would be their partner tonight. The girls danced together until excused by two lads from one of the villages and if the partnership worked you spent the rest of the evening together — and in a lot of cases the rest of your life. How many of today's teenagers have grandparents who met in this way?

The following evening you could repeat the process once again at the Edwinstowe Rendezvous. You had to have a little yellow membership card to gain entrance there and the music was supplied by a DJ.

Enid Johnson

DAY-LEWIS

The Reverend Frank Day-Lewis came to Edwinstowe in 1918 when it was a farming community. He turned the Lady Chapel into a memorial to the dead of the Great War and conducted the annual Armistice Day ceremony at the War Memorial.

His son, Cecil, wrote detective novels under name of Nicholas Blake. There is a character named Edwin Stowe in one of them!

(**SEE ALSO:** CECIL DAY-LEWIS BY DENNIS WOOD ON PAGE 24)

DONKEY RACES

These were held in November 1841, at the same time as the Forest Gatherings, as part of the Edwinstowe Races: "A new bridle will be run for by Jerusalem Donkeys of all ages. The second Neddy to be presented with a crupper as a reward for his not being too forward in the race. No crossing, jostling or braying of any kind will be allowed."

Other attractions included: "The juvenile who should best display his agility by climbing to the top of a nicely buttered high pole" would win a new beaver hat. "Bobbing for oranges, cuts for the comical through a collar and other rural sports for valuable purses." Visitors were entertained with meals, theatrical performances, assembly rooms and concerts in the village.

(**SOURCE:** *RETFORD & GAINSBOROUGH TIMES*)

Cecil Day-Lewis

Cecil Day-Lewis was born in Ballintubbert, Ireland, on 27th April 1904, the son of Frank Cecil Day-Lewis, a Church of Ireland curate, who had married Kathleen Blake Squires. That Cecil should achieve literary fame may well be attributed to his claim to some illustrious forebears. His maternal grandmother was a Goldsmith, directly descended from the uncle of Oliver Goldsmith, and another branch of his mother's family can be traced to the Brontës, whose father grew up in County Down. Cecil's paternal grandmother, a Butler, may have been related to William Butler Yeats.

While Cecil was a baby, his father was appointed curate of a priory in Malvern, and Cecil has committed to verse an incident when his mother stopped his pram beside a lake:

"The bells that chimed beside the lake,
  The swans asleep in evening's eye,
  Bright transfers pressed on memory:
From him their gloss and anguish take."

His father moved to Ealing and Cecil was to suffer a child's greatest anguish. He was taken into a room where his mother was lying. He was placed in her arms and she kissed him. It was the last time he saw her. (As a hospital nurse she was known as 'The Angel'.)

Her sister, Agnes Olive Squires, 'Knos', became his surrogate mother for 12 years "with a devotion few other women could have equalled".

In his youth and beyond he was nervous in company because, in childhood, he had been isolated from other children, Knos being responsible for his early education. He confessed to a poor memory, this self-conscious trait causing him to entitle his autobiography *The Buried Day*.

Cecil's father at times distanced himself from his upbringing and Cecil must have felt like an orphan, but he enjoyed blissful holidays with Knos in Ireland at Monart Rectory, the home of her brother, a rector. Uncle Willie, "silent as a Trappist", and eccentric, was kind, patient and generous. Knos aroused in Cecil an interest in music, singing arias from Handel's *Messiah* and popular songs of the time. Cecil could pick up a melody and had a mellifluous voice. He once took part "in an *Irish Half Hour* broadcast with the great John McCormack, an adorable man with a heart of gold". Cecil was made a member of the Incorporated Society of Musicians. Keyes, his uncle Willie's gardener, taught him to identify flowers and insects.

Cecil's father served as a curate at Ealing and Notting Hill and then at Lancaster Gate, from 1910. "My father was handsome, gentlemanly and a widower. Some women parishioners believed that the best way to his heart was through his son's stomach, and they plied me with sweets."

"Father was tolerant of my childish pranks," he wrote, "and he had a relaxed attitude to my religious duties. Knos and I attended Matins but I never went to Sunday school and there were few Sabbath prohibitions. There were family prayers, and grace before meals was taken for granted. After lunch Knos and I would walk in Kensington Gardens."

Cecil was 14 when his father was appointed Vicar of Edwinstowe. In *The Buried Day* Cecil reminisces: "When my father moved to Edwinstowe it was a country village. Before he died it had become a mining town. For all our sylvan surroundings I was made aware that it was a colliery district. The acrid smell of slag-tips overcast the scent of our summer roses... I could hear the distant rattle of the pit-head winding gear — the only sound, except for a jay screeching or rooks cawing, which broke the brooding silences of the ancient woodland... Soon the new housing estates were to obliterate the contours of the fields, which, as a boy, I had seen tossing with wheat or barley."

He recalls that his father's stipend of £600 per annum came largely from the titled patron of the living, beneath whose land the coal had been found. Earl Manvers was one of four noblemen whose ancestors had enclosed part of Sherwood Forest and given the district its name of the Dukeries.

Although Cecil claimed to have been "socially insulated" in Edwinstowe, John Manning, a lifetime resident, who was baptised by Cecil's father, asserts that Cecil did occasionally play tennis with his mother, Hilda Digby, and her friend, Annie Parnell.

Cecil's father was very class-conscious; Cecil was not allowed to join the church choir or the Boy Scouts because the boys were not of his class.

In his 50s the idea of eternal life filled him with horror and revolt and he repudiated his father's faith. He had gradually lapsed into agnosticism in his youth and he never recovered from it. However, he wrote later, "I still, on my churchless evenings, feel a vague depression and unconsciously start singing a hymn. I've found my poems taking a religious turn. As a child I loved my father without reservation."

Henry Cartledge, one of the few Edwinstowe villagers who can remember the vicar, says: "He was the traditional disciplinarian, aloof, conscious of his role and position in society." This attitude would thrive in his London parish where he numbered the Lord Mayor among his congregation.

Cecil qualified for Sherborne, a public school, where the Reverend Henry Robinson King, whose daughter he was to marry, instilled in him a liking for English poetry by reading aloud Wordsworth and Tennyson. He scribbled away in spare moments, a heterodox activity that was tolerated by fellow pupils because of his prowess at rugby. There were times when he was flooded with a radiant sense of peace:

"The truth of flesh and spirit, sun and clay,
Singing for once together, all in tune."

His achievements were many: he commanded the PE squad, which won the Public Schools' Shield. His membership of the oratorio choir and the more select chapel choir helped him win a singing prize. He was appointed prefect and head of house. He edited the school magazine and dared to write a leading article censuring the poor attendance of masters at choir practice.

Cecil was entertained by the school doctor, "who gave us wine and adult conversation in judicious doses." He drove the Principal in his car on Sunday afternoons.

In 1921 Cecil's father married Mamie Wilkinson and Cecil was given leave from Sherborne to act as best man. His relationship with his father deteriorated, shattering the father–son bond, which had been so full of joy. His father would often lapse into sulks and rages and could never express contrition. Cecil became increasingly sceptical of his father's unchristian views, a feeling exacerbated upon hearing clergymen discussing the stipends or shortcomings of their colleagues.

Although he sang in the choir and read lessons at St Mary's his disenchantment kept him away from Holy Communion, a sacrament that no longer meant anything to him.

His summer visits to Trent Bridge evoked the embryonic poet: "Harold Larwood's run-up to the wicket, its smooth, almost imperceptible acceleration, and the legato movement in delivery, remains one of the most beautiful displays of bodily grace I've ever seen."

In Sherwood, Cecil's love of nature flourished: he contrasts alliteratively the Sherwood oaks, "romantic, rotting, riven by lightning", with the "raw, regimented lines of conifers".

He was an enlightened and observant witness of the changing times. With prophetic insight he realised that the miners were in the forefront of a transformation that would lead the country out of the dismal days of the 1930s to sustain the war effort on the home front and in the front line, and revitalise the post-war economy. At the dawn of the 21st century the colliery still produces coal in abundance. Remote though the village miners' lives were from him, it was in Edwinstowe that his social conscience was born. He felt he was being poisoned by his solitary upbringing, which prevented him from making contact with other people. I wonder whether this is the facet in his character that makes some of his verse difficult to understand. Was he marooned in his own version of the English language?

Aged 18 or 19, Cecil experienced periodical black moods. Mary King rescued him. She was loyal and affectionate, evoking tenderness in Cecil. They read poetry together and when she stayed in the vicarage, his father accepted her. At Mary's house he enjoyed her father's incomparable readings of Jane Austen, Dickens and Thackeray.

Cecil won a scholarship to Wadham College, Oxford, on the strength of his English essay. Cecil's sheltered upbringing had inhibited his natural growth. Gradually, however, he embraced the ancient Greek admonition, "Know thyself!" and, in the intellectual climate of Oxford, his wits quickened and flowered and his undoubted charisma came to the fore, endearing him to many of his companions. He made friends with many scholars and literary giants, among whom were John Betjeman, Nancy Mitford, David Cecil and L A G Strong, and he became very attached to Charles Fenby and Rex Warner. Cecil also made a great friend of Sir Maurice Bowra, Dean of Wadham. That he should one day succeed Sir Maurice as Oxford Professor of Poetry was beyond his wildest dreams, for "my own academic incompetence was becoming ever plainer to me".

From 1925 Cecil published verse, though often suffering the pain of rejection. At Wadham he joined a literary society called *Jawbone*, becoming secretary and president. "We were all aspiring writers and real writers addressed us: Strong, Wolfe, Laurence Binyon and Robert Graves, who detected some promise in my first *Book of Poems*".

After his final exam in Classics, Cecil taught for a year at Summer Fields, a preparatory school where L A G Strong was teaching. He married Mary in 1928 and taught briefly at Helensburgh, Scotland. He then moved to Cheltenham Public School, teaching English and Classics until 1935.

In the 1930s he was politically active, writing for the *Left Review*, supporting the *Left Book Club*, and he briefly joined the Communist Party. These interests are apparent in *Transitional Poem*, *From Feathers to Iron* and *The Magnetic Mountain*, but he achieved more success when he moved to poems of a more personal nature.

From Feathers to Iron relates his own experience before the birth of his first child, Sean. His own excitement and apprehension linked up spontaneously with the struggle and the joy in which a new world should be born. In 1938 he and Mary moved to Musbury, Devon. He wrote lyrically: "The floors of copses smoked with bluebells, as if fires were burning underground, and we walked down our lane between ribbons and rosettes of red and white and gold. In the garden the daffodils trumpeted to the sun in incense-breathing morn."

In the 1930s, Cecil embarked on a separate career as a detective novelist, under the pseudonym of Nicholas Blake. Shut away seven days a week, writing, he gradually grew apart from Mary, though they had time to entertain distinguished writers who came to address the Cheltenham Literary Society, of which he was president. He fell from grace by indulging in an extra-marital affair and Mary and he were divorced. Cecil left Musbury suffering an agony of heart.

Cecil's reputation was enhanced through membership of the Auden-Spender-Day Lewis School. They didn't know they were a movement until critics told them they were. In 1934, T.E. Lawrence is reported to have told Winston Churchill that Cecil was a good prospect.

Cecil commanded a troop in the Home Guard and then moved to London to work in the Ministry of Information in 1939. In the 1940s he learned to see poetry everywhere, "in the most commonplace things and in the precious strata of my past experience."

In 1959 he married Jill Balcon. They had two children, Daniel, well known as an actor, and Tamasin. When they were young they had to respect his privacy when he was in his study, a hallowed room. Tamasin recalls how helpful her father was with her homework, especially with English Literature.

In 1968, upon John Masefield's death, Cecil Day-Lewis succeeded him as Poet Laureate, a court official appointed by the Prime Minister (Harold Wilson at the time).

Cecil's widow, Jill, recalls that, during the power failures of 1971, when he was skeleton thin and dying of cancer, she laid a fire to keep him warm: "I'm always on the side of the miners," he said. Cecil composed his own postscript to this tribute: "I hope that, when I come to die, if I have still no belief in immortality, I may at least recapture the docility of the child I once was, and go into the dark with an acquiescent murmur."

Dennis Wood

Reverend Frank Cecil Day-Lewis conducting the Armistice Service at the War Memorial in 1929

EDWARD, PRINCE OF WALES
(later KING EDWARD VII)

Queen Victoria's eldest son regularly stayed at Rufford Abbey when he visited Doncaster Races. Rufford school-children lined up outside the Abbey to sing the National Anthem to greet him. The following day he would visit the school and distribute slices of cake, after which the schol-ars had a half-day holiday.

The royal train, resplendent with royal coat of arms, would arrive on the 'wrong' platform at Ollerton so that the royal party did not have to cross the footbridge.

EDWINSTOWE CARRIAGE OWNERS
ASSOCIATION

Formed in 1897 under the chairmanship of Mr Naish, the proprietor of the Royal Oak public house, to provide trans-port for visitors arriving at Edwinstowe Station. They travelled by four-in-hand or wagonette along Mansfield Road via Clipstone to Rufford Park. After a refreshment stop at the Jug & Glass or Dukeries Hotel they visited the Major Oak. They then went around the grounds of Thoresby Hall via Greyhound Lodge, Clumber Bridge and Lime Tree Avenue. Operators had keys to the grounds of the ducal estates. In 1898 the Duke of Portland threatened to close his estate because these conveyances were dan-gerously overcrowded.

The Dragonfly's Song

Harsh winter cowers in the light of approaching sun
Ragged, wind wrenched boughs, skeletal against the sky
Winter gropes to destroy what it cannot keep,
Whilst I lie in the mud, and wait.

Valiant wind driven clouds
Whistle in storm ridden throng
Winter clings to the hills
Determined to keep holding on.
But I lie in the mud and wait.

Carnivorous I;
Skin shedding nymph
Safe in my watery home
As winter gropes to destroy what it cannot keep.
Still! I lie in the mud and wait.

When battle is o'er and winter is slain
I crawl from my mud-soft bed.
At the kiss of a Dawn
By the banks of the Maun
I climb the tall grass lane.
Bursting of skin
Spreading of wing
My jewel-like glory I show.
Carnivorous I;
Highflying dragonfly
Dancing with sunbeams
Awaiting a mate.

Sheila Norton

FAIR

In 1381, under a Royal Charter, an Annual Fair was granted on the Vigil and Day of St Eadwin (around 24th October). A toll was given to the church.

Older villagers today have fond memories of riding on the roundabouts (cranky horses) when the fair arrived each year. Having occupied several sites around the village, the present-day fairground on the edge of Sherwood Forest is under the management of the Turvill family, who have been associated with the fair for over 200 years.

FIREWORK FACTORY

A large magazine and seven huts were sited on an acre of land near Lidgett House and 'Bombes' became a popular part of most local festivities. The factory closed around 1900. The owner, George Pindar, was injured by an explosion, but later exhibited scientific experiments in a tent.

FOREST LAWS

In the Middle Ages, Sherwood Forest covered 100,000 acres. Edwinstowe tenants were freeborn, royal manor dwellers who enjoyed privileges: gathering underwood, pannage (grazing pigs on acorns and beech mast).

The Forest Laws were a punishment code imposed by the king on local people who broke strict rules protecting timber and game. Minor offenders were put on the

Verderer's list and brought before an attachment court, which was held every seven weeks in the village.

FOREST GATHERINGS

In November 1841 literary figures came from Sheffield and Derbyshire to enjoy feasting and poetry in the forest. It was so enjoyable that it was repeated in1842. An enormous tent was erected on the Forest-side and about 500 people attended.

(**SOURCE:** *SPENCER HALL SKETCHES OF REMARKABLE PEOPLE*)

Growing up in a Mining Village in the 1930s and 1940s

2. Mam

My mam, as most of the miners' wives, was the hub or our household, the very centre of everything that was going on.

She was always there for us, pottering about busy with her daily chores, one ear cocked to the radio. Her first job in the morning and her last at night was to flick the knob of the wireless. She was an absolute devotee, but we learned to switch off our minds to all the music and talk, and could easily hold long involved family conversations to this joyous accompaniment of my mam's day. Life was hard for housewives in those days, no wonderful gadgets to help speed away the monotonous hard work of their daily lives.

The daily grind was made doubly hard for my mother. As a tiny tot of four years she had been the victim of a dreadful accident and on her fifth birthday she had gone under the surgeon's knife to have a leg amputated.

What a traumatic shock that must have been, not only to the poor child, but also to her whole family.

At that time help for the poorer classes toward rehabilitation was practically unheard of and certainly restricted to charitable aid.

To while away the long hours of pain and discomfort she became accomplished with the sewing needle and could make her knitting needles clatter along at a terrific pace. These skills had been passed to her by her mother and she in her turn passed them down to Lucy and myself.

Although I was taught to sew, I never enjoyed it, finding hemming and darting wearisome tasks and I abandoned these skills at the earliest opportunity.

Lucy, not such a fidget as I, became as excellent as mam at the art of dressmaking and knitting. These were skills

35

that came in useful when she had three daughters of her own to clothe.

I found I could read and knit at the same time, now here was something that I could enjoy, the garment grew and I could still pursue my favourite pastime.

It was not unusual in our house to find three of us sitting on hard chairs around the kitchen table, knitting the most complex patterns with reading books propped up before us. When I was in the babies' class at school, the girls were given a set of small knitting needles and a tiny ball of rainbow coloured wool. We were to be taught to knit. I can remember thinking I can already do this, so up went my hand.

"Please Miss. I can already knit."

"Yes, dear, I am sure you can, but I'll show you how we do it at school."

Lesson commenced and I was away. I cast on the stitches, knitted, purled, cast off and in no time - Hey presto! — A small piece of knitting accomplished.

After that I was allowed to bring in my own knitting, which at that time was a scarf in the most intricate lacy pattern that my mother had taught me by rote.

I must have seemed a real know-all to the rest of the girls and the teacher.

Times were still hard, but when I was about six years old, my mam had saved enough to purchase wool for two jumper suits with mock pleated skirts, one was red and the other green. I was proud as punch and wore them constantly until I outgrew them.

Mam then painstakingly unpicked them and knitted the reclaimed wool into two jumpers, which I wore until my elbows were showing. Not to be outdone, they were unpicked and this time transformed into warm mittens.

During the war I was in desperate need of a warm winter coat, so mam put her skills to use and turned a grey army blanket into the desired garment.

My mam was a very thrifty lady indeed.

In Edwinstowe House, which was quite near our

Avenue, lived the family of the Managing Director of Bolsover Colliery Company. They had a daughter, Diana, the same age as me.

We had met occasionally whilst playing at the dyke near the boundary of their mansion. We children thought Diana was a very lucky girl; beautiful clothes, big house, swimming pool, pony, handsome brother and doting parents. Who could ask for more?

One day I espied a vision of loveliness. Blond, curly haired Diana on her way to church dressed in the most delightful pink satin dress with three frills on the skirt. I was entranced at this vision of beauty, and described the dress in full detail to my mam. Imagine my delight when some little time later I was given a wonderful surprise from my mam — she had made me a replica of the dress, perhaps not in satin but nevertheless very beautiful. I was a princess, even though I had straight hair, freckles and a dumpy figure.

In all her life my mam never owned a sewing machine. All her work was done by hand.

I may not have been dressed to Dior standards, but I was as well turned out, with satin ribbons in my hair, as my mam could make me.

During the war all the miners' wives made wonderful meals from practically nothing. Meat and potato pie was our favourite. Ted and I would rush home from school to partake of this scrumptious feast. Friday brought cod and parsley sauce, peas and potatoes to the table, treacle suet pudding, and rice pudding with the skin on top. A special treat was rabbit stew; Ted and I fell out many times over this delicacy. But we hated washdays, as all the schoolchildren did. Instead of scampering, we dawdled home at lunchtime. We would be greeted with a very hot, irate mother.

"Where have you been? You're late. Turn the washer handle 35 times and put that pile of washing through the mangle please, whilst I put this washing on the line."

Ted would often plead some life-threatening injury to

free him from these loathsome tasks but mam was a wise lady and would brook no idleness from either of us.

Mam would return from the washing line to dish up cold meat, tinned peas and bubble and squeak and no pudding. What a horrible day.

It was of no consequence to Ted and me that mam had been up from the crack of dawn, washing, mangling, boiling whites and pegging out on the line. And, horror of horrors, if it rained all the washing had to be dried indoors on clotheshorses around the fires, making the whole house damp and dreary.

The washing of pit clothes was the final job of the washing machine. Incidentally, this was a hand-driven nightmare, not electric as the modern ones of today.

The filthy, horrible apparel worn by my dad in the pit, had to be banged vigorously against the outside wall to help release the dust, and then into the washer with them. The stench released was horrific, but this nauseous task had to be undertaken every week. No collier's wife worth her salt would let her husband go to the pit in clothes that had been sullied for more than a week.

Washday was a weekly nightmare to be endured. Nowhere to go out of the way to read or play.

These events would be replicated in most houses around us. The children would return to school after dinnertime with doleful faces.

It would not be much better when we returned later, our mothers would be so exhausted after their horrendous day that they had no inclination to listen to our events of the day. It was almost a relief to be packed off to bed.

I was born in 1931, the third daughter in the family, and I imagine that a baby was the last thing in the world that my parents needed, when times were still hard and work was short at Thoresby. Nevertheless I was as welcome as my siblings were.

My first real memory was, as little more than a baby, sitting in my pram being wheeled to the 'New Shop' (so-called because it had been built on the Estate). I was left outside to be cooed over by passers by whilst my mother purchased her scant provisions.

No caring mother in today's society would dare to leave their child in such a vulnerable position, but times were very different then, when everyone cared for each other, and most children were treasured by all.

My eldest sister Elsie was born in 1919 with a learning disability and was never able to go to work. She was a loving, pretty and charming girl, who never grew up. She was a tremendous help to my mother and was sadly missed by all when she died of meningitis at the age of 23. I was 11 at the time and Lucy was 22.

Lucy, my other sister, born in 1920, was recommended by the school for work as a lady's maid in a mansion in London. The lady paid my sister's train fare and off she went to the great Metropolis at the tender age of 14.

In today's society she would still have been classed as a child. Fortunately my mother had a sister married to a Londoner who lived in the great city, so Lucy was able to spend some time with family on her very meagre time off.

I was only three, but I clearly remember the distress in our home at the parting from their young daughter. I sorely missed my loving playmate and nursemaid.

The ordeal did not last for long. Lucy was terribly homesick and after a few months my distraught parents decided that dad should fetch her home.

She was given excellent references and therefore soon found a position as a parlourmaid in Nottingham. Again she lived away from home but was able to visit us on her days off. My mother took me to visit her on several occasions.

Mrs Goodwin, the proprietor of the boarding house in which Lucy worked, made us very welcome and made it clear to my mam that she was very pleased with Lucy and her work.

A highlight of one of these visits was being given a huge block of Cadbury's chocolate by one of the commercial travellers, a jovial fellow, who lived in the house.

What a wonderful treat. Ecstasy! I could not wait to get home to share this delicious chocolate with Ted, who of course received it in his usual laid-back fashion, but I know this was just his way and he enjoyed it as much as I.

Pam and her brother Ted (c. 1941)

We munched that chocolate for days and our dreams at night were of eating the next square. In modern parlance we were "chocolated out!"

When a textile factory was built at New Ollerton, Lucy rejoined her family and became an ironer of ladies underwear, a job she loved and continued to do until she married and left to be a housewife. I used to think, 'What a chore!' I know I certainly would have hated ironing all day long. Paid manual work was not in my scheme of things for the future.

Pam Bird

40

G

GAS WORKS

In 1844 Miles Webster on the High Street installed gas lighting in his home and the Jug and Glass next door, plus a light on the street. The rest of the village didn't have street lamps until 1893.

Talking Heads

Visitors to St Mary's Church, Edwinstowe, often ask to be shown something from Robin Hood's time, so I take them along the centre aisle and round the Lady Chapel pointing out my favourite carved heads.

Some are superb, others quite crudely carved. There's a rude giant sticking out his tongue to scare off the devil, Thomas Becket glowering across at King Henry, a glum bishop, an improbable angel, some ladies in fashionable headgear and a poor little ET look-alike hiding up in the corner by the font.

In the Lady Chapel the oddest-looking carved head has dead straight hair, one eye higher than the other and what appears to be a brooch under her double chin. One day I was watching some slides of Southwell Minster when to my great surprise a similar face appeared on the screen. The speaker said, "This is St Katherine and that's her wheel."

As soon as I got home I looked up Katherine of Alexandria in my dictionary of saints. I couldn't believe the incredibly ugly face was supposed to portray a saint! In the middle ages St Katherine and St Margaret were more popular than the Apostles, especially with young women like Joan of Arc who went to the stake still claiming they had told her to wear men's clothing and fight the English.

There's a rather unflattering statue of Margaret of Antioch in Edwinstowe's Lady Chapel, which is dedicated to her. The contract for the priests serving the double chantry gives us some idea of the importance of these two virgin martyrs around 1342:

"...every Custos of the said altar shall every day — except on Double feasts and Sundays, and on the festival of Saint Katherine and Saint Margaret Virgins — say Mass of the Blessed Virgin......"

Thanks to the Internet I also discovered an important link with Southwell Minster — the manuscript of St Athanasius's eyewitness report of Katherine's colourful adventures. Since Henry de Edenstou, one of the chantry priests, was also a prebendery of Southwell Minster, it's not difficult to guess how similar carvings of St Katherine come to be in the two churches.

Although the Vatican abolished her feast day in the 1960s, judging by the number of St Katherine websites, she still has many young women admirers.

Liz Stewart-Smith

HALL

Edwinstowe Hall, on Church Street, was built in the early part of the 18th century. It has a fine plaster ceiling in the Rococo manner with cherubs in low relief on the central panel. The two-storey drawing room dates from 1751. It is now a respite home.

Two Haiku

Owl resting upon
Ancient oak of the forest
Death awaits the mouse

North winds blow in the forest
Many trees will fall
The Oak remains unmoved.

Sheila Norton

Our Edwinstowe

We know the tales of Robin Hood,
And all the things that he did good.
We know about the old oak tree,
That stands in the forest for all to see.
But how are we ever to recall,
The grand old building that stood proud and tall,
Where gatherings of people would be seen
To watch their heroes on the big screen?
How are we to remember that,
When all that's left is a block of flats?
Rufford school shared the same fate,
Another building demolished of late.
The only memories of that we've found
Are to make way for a building ground.
Put new homes there in its place,
Don't worry that there's no learning space.
Edwinstowe's growing, it's plain to see,
All this will go down in history.
The old welfare, the leisure centre too,
Making way for all things new.
So what does the future hold
For our village, our town, our Edwinstowe?

Betty Ann Glover

I

INSTITUTE

Situated on the High Street, the Institute was donated in 1913 for the young men in the village by Earl Manvers, providing board games and a reading room. Women were not allowed! In 1951 it became the Library. Now it's the Adult Education Centre.

Life as a Volunteer Sheep Warden

"One, two, three, four, five — stay where you are! Six, seven — don't move! Oh, OK, two, four, five, eight, ten over there... three — or is it four? — lying down over there....."

No, I'm not counting sheep to try and get to sleep — I'm actually counting real sheep, part of a large flock of rare Hebridean sheep being used to graze areas of Sherwood Forest as part of a conservation grazing project being run by Nottinghamshire Wildlife Trust.

My job as a volunteer sheep warden simply involves checking a group of around 30 sheep as often as I can manage — counting them to make sure there are none missing, and generally having a good look at them to check for potential problems. My knowledge of sheep is somewhat limited, but at least I can look out for any that are limping or look unwell, and report any problems to the shepherd.

Of course, I have to find them first, which is not always easy, as they roam over a fairly large area and seem to delight in hiding from me — at least until I've walked all the way around their fenced enclosure and am back where I started.

Hebridean sheep are being used by the Nottinghamshire Wildlife Trust to help manage a range of heathlands and grasslands to improve the quality of wildlife habitat, and the so-called "Flying Flock" was established in 1999 with the purchase of 70 sheep.

Sensitive grazing is now accepted to be the most practical effective means of managing heathland and helping to protect its fragile ecosystem, and Hebrideans are highly suited to beneficial grazing of unimproved vegetation and heathland. In addition to working on heathland sites, including Rainworth Heath and parts of Clumber Park, the flock has allowed the Trust to reinstate traditional management on a number of important wildflower meadows where plants such as cowslip, hay rattle and orchids grow.

The sheep trample and eat coarse grasses, scrub and young tree seedlings, exposing areas of bare ground where new seeds are able to take hold and develop, thereby helping to encourage heather and fine grasses on the heathland and increasing the number of fine grasses and wildflowers on the meadows. Areas of undernourished soil are ideal for wildflowers. Bare ground is also vital for invertebrates, which need to burrow to lay eggs, or establish areas in which to catch prey.

Hebridean sheep are considered to be one of the most reliable and effective breeds for use in conservation grazing schemes. As a result, the breed, which had almost died out, now has a healthy and growing population, with flocks across the UK. The Nottinghamshire Wildlife Trust flock is now one of the largest pure-bred flocks in the world — the flock currently consists of over 600 sheep, distributed across more than 30 sites around Nottinghamshire and looked after by a full-time shepherd — and several volunteers!

The sheep were introduced into an area of Sherwood Forest near Edwinstowe in 2003, to try to control erosion of the heathland. A large fenced area was made available for them, although this does not restrict public access. A further fenced area is to be added in 2005, increasing the grazed area to around 220 acres, or 50% of the park. Grazing is an established forest management tool — over time this ancient forest will resemble, even more closely, how it looked in medieval times.

Sara Hulse

J

JUG AND GLASS

A Victorian public house on the High Street. It was home
to the Penny Library in 1838. It had the first gas lighting
in Edwinstowe and an early telephone (SEE: TELEPHONE
EXCHANGE). Before the First World War it provided lunches
for the four-in-hand coaches, which carried 20 adults at a
time on the Dukeries Tour.

Heartless

I gave you my heart to keep,
And you lost it.

You said it was
Around here somewhere,
With all the other things you didn't need.

You looked under the bed
And found a broken fragment
Distorted by dust,
Another, pricking at the back of your mind
And another, clinging to the sleeve
Of the red sweater you bought me for Valentines.

You tried to fix it back together,
Hoping I wouldn't notice the cracks.
But even superglue couldn't get us
To stick it out.

When I said I was leaving,
You said I was heartless.

But not quite,
I carried enough in my bag
To start again.

Sue Allen

Men are like Bras

Men are like bras,
they start off firm
and supportive, giving
form and foundation to
your life.

But soon they start to lose
the point, turning into
grey and saggy,
threadbare reflections
of their former selves.

The material falls into
holes in your hands,
as you contemplate the
ultimate disappointment
of elasticated passion.

Let down and droopy
just when you needed some
uplift in your life.

Let that be a lesson to you.
Never trust anyone
who says:
"Cross my heart."

Sue Allen

KINGS STAND FARM

Kings Stand Farm on the outskirts of Edwinstowe (going towards Ollerton), is said to be where the King would wait for the deer to be driven towards him during the hunt. Similar sites are at Cuckney and Berry Hill.

KITCHEN, FRED (1891-1969)

Born in Edwinstowe, Fred Kitchen wrote *Brother to the Ox* (1940), which describes his life as a farmhand. He also wrote *Songs of Sherwood* (1948).

KINGS CLIPSTONE

The ruins of the royal hunting lodge, which had stabling for more than 200 horses — it is now known as King John's Palace. King Edward I held Parliament at Clipstone in 1290. It was used regularly until the 14th century.

Growing up in a Mining Village in the 1930s and 1940s

3. School

Schools are always at the heart of any community, and so it was at that time in Edwinstowe. There were now two schools in the village, the original, educating approximately 90 children, was a Church school, having been endowed by Earl Manvers in the late 19th century. To this day the Thoresby Estate directors remain patrons of the voluntary-aided school, which was rebuilt in 1969.

The original building stands on Mansfield Road, and still plays a vital part in the community as Village Hall and Parish Council office.

The Church school building consisted of a large room divided by folding wooden shutters in which the junior and senior children were taught. The infant classroom was light and airy, having been added to the building at a later date.

The whole school was heated by mighty dragons of black, pot-bellied stoves surrounded by huge metal fire-guards belching out fearsome heat and fumes, warming the fronts of the classrooms, whilst those poor mites at the back shivered and shook in icy conditions. Two tiny cloak-rooms, outdoor lavatories and a small playground completed the school facilities.

The later, much more palatial school, with which I was more familiar, having spent many years there, had been built on the fringe of the new colliery housing estate to mainly house the large influx of miners' children.

The brick-built Council School was set in spacious grounds, with playing fields to the front and back, and playgrounds to each side. Again, as in the 'old school', the lavatories were outside; boys in one yard, girls in another.

The internal layout was similar to all the recent schools built in the new colliery villages. Ours comprised two long intersecting corridors, flanked on one side by classrooms, with windows on the other side and cloakrooms with hot and cold water.

A school hall fulfilled many functions — assembly, indoor games, PE, concerts and, during the war, the facility was let out to dance classes in the evening. The whole building was made as warm as toast by central heating fuelled by coal from the local mines.

The first sign of the antagonism between the old and new village now became apparent in the behaviour of the pupils towards each other. They were sworn enemies. We looked with disdain upon the children from the 'old school', while they treated us with great animosity. Is there any wonder there is so much strife and division in the world, when the prejudices of parents are so obviously transferred to their children?

Boys from the 'old school' descended on our school every Friday to be taught in the woodwork room, while the girls took over the Domestic Science room. They must have been mortified to be treading on enemy territory.

However, as always in life, the Friday invasion became routine for both schools and was soon accepted by the pupils, if not by their parents.

Fortunately, as time evolved, several children from the 'old village' were admitted to our school, and similarly miners' children were taken on the roll of the Church School. It took many years before these antagonistic scars were healed and all — or most — of the children and their parents, from both ends of the village, finally buried their differences and came to understand, acknowledge and accept the new order of things.

The rule in the Council School was that if a pupil should wish to use the lavatories during lesson time the child had to raise a hand and wait for the teacher to allow the pupil concerned to leave the room. Depending on how benevolent the teacher felt, or how quickly you were noticed, it was often a desperate flight to get there in time, especially in the winter when outer clothing had to be donned before venturing outside. I suspect many of us had 'accidents' that we were too embarrassed to reveal to our peers at the time.

These lavatories were an endless source of innocent entertainment to us. At playtime we would often gather round them and with much screaming and hysteria play 'tag' with the boys. We knew 'sudden death' awaited us if the teacher on playground duty found boys chasing girls in the lavs, but nevertheless the games continued for years until the toilet facilities were finally rebuilt and moved indoors during the 1980s.

The girls always 'went' together — we were practically joined at the hip to our best friends, so we continued our nattering while performing our bodily functions. Even today you will often see young women go off to the loo together, enabling them to continue chatting through the dividing partitions.

The children usually started school at the beginning of the term in which they became five years old, leaving fully educated to the standards of the time at the tender age of fourteen.

I was four years and nine months when my first day in school dawned. I had been scrubbed until my skin glowed. Polished shoes and clean dress were the order of the day.

I remember trotting happily by my mam's side, holding her comfortable and familiar hand. Taking me into the baby's room, mam left me under the watchful eye of dear Mrs Staniland, a dedicated and patient teacher, who overflowed with love of children.

Having been given a slate and pencil (wonderful, unexpected gifts) I was quite happy to sit there on my small wooden chair, chin cupped in one hand, elbows on table, watching the interesting events unfolding before me in the busy room.

Never having been in a classroom before, I was quite fascinated by the interesting projects that were being undertaken by the far superior children, who had started school before me. Presently we were all given a small bottle of milk, which the teacher had thoughtfully warmed on the hot pipes. This was a treat indeed and the contents were quickly consumed, with the aid of a drinking straw.

I had never seen one of these novelties before. So, not wanting to appear stupid, I watched carefully while the other children pierced a hole in the cardboard stopper in the milk bottle top enabling them to insert a straw. Right, I had learned the procedure! Not so! First, thumb into hole in top of bottle. Second, straw into bottle. Third, other end into mouth and suck. Easy? Of course. But my inexperienced thumb slipped into the milk and a cascade of the delicious nectar showered over me.

Was I in trouble? Of course not. The milk monitor for the day soon mopped me up, so I did not bother to cry after all. Instead I thought, "What an interesting time I'm having at school."

Playtime came next, when we were allowed into the playground with our friends to run around for a few minutes.

Of course, I didn't know any other child at that time so feeling a mite lonely, and knowing my mam was at home, I decided that I'd enjoyed school but now was a good time to finish my education and go home to play in familiar places.

On the way the call of nature I had been ignoring for some time got the better of me, and so a little girl with wet panties arrived home just a little crestfallen and tearful. After a quick change and a cuddle with my mam, back I went to be met by a concerned but understanding teacher.

I soon found my little niche in this new and exciting world and never played hookey again.

It was in these young and formative infant years that our lifelong friendships were developed. My special friend Beryl and I were inseparable companions; she had freckles, bright red hair and a temper to match. I also had the freckles and was constantly on a short fuse, as a consequence we had many heated arguments over all manner of illogical things. There would be a minor explosion of words, but never fisticuffs, and off we would flounce to our respective homes, vowing never to speak to each other again. The tantrum never lasted more than two hours before one or the other was knocking at the door.

"Are you coming out to play?"

These tiffs lasted well into our teenage years, but of course we were now disagreeing about the really important issues touching our lives — hairdos, boys, lipsticks, clothes, music, who we should or should not allow to dance with us.

Siamese twins had nothing on us. My mam said that we were the worst friends and best enemies she had ever known. We remained inseparable until the inevitable happened, when Beryl met the love of her life and married him at the age of 19. Con whisked her off to live in London, and I seldom saw her in the following years.

Beryl and I never intended to be disruptive, but somehow we got into all kinds of scrapes together, and always seemed to be at odds with authority, both at school and home. We must have been a constant source of stress to our parents.

We were both caned across our hands on several occasions, usually for talking in class — a great crime in those days. Not to talk for hours on end was a nightmare to chatterboxes like us; we therefore often broke the silence with a whisper or two. We were nearly always caught. Inevitably, because we were somewhat unruly, we were often blamed and were scapegoats for misdemeanours that we had not committed. We both felt very ill judged at times, but we survived.

When leaving school in the past, most of the boys had followed their dads into the mines. The girls were often put into 'service', as my sister Lucy had been. However, long before it came time for me to leave school I considered 'service' a horrible demeaning job, and had no intention of getting caught up in wearing a frilly cap and apron. A resolution I am glad to say I was fortunate in being able to keep.

However, times were rapidly changing. The miners and their wives — having made the first giant stride forward in their own lives — wanted better opportunities for their children. They discovered that scholarships were available in the county, which enabled some of the children to gain admittance to grammar schools, technical colleges and other further education establishments.

Competition was great for the few places available, but the children of Edwinstowe, both from the old and new schools, took up the challenge and went on to hone their educational skills in these rarefied establishments. This was tutoring for various professions unheard of previously for the children of miners, farm workers and estate workers.

In the fullness of time they became solicitors, teachers, officers in the armed forces, nurses, doctors, engineers, electricians, musicians, administrators, colliery managers and officials. Many other key jobs were obtained by these dedicated and groundbreaking children of the working class. A far cry indeed from the days of the lowly position in the pecking order of society.

Meanwhile, the strong backbone and salt of the earth of all communities, the young people going to work for the first time as miners, farm labourers, factory workers and shop assistants had been educated by both parents and forward looking teachers to realise that they too had a valued place in society and could work to realise their own potential for a better future. Robin Hood had certainly stood by his word to help the poor in Sherwood Forest.

The children of Edwinstowe had come far and were on the way upward, taking the village with them — albeit on a long and tortuous path.

The head teacher in the Church School was for many years Mr Firth, while in the council school two head teachers were at the helm, Mr Perry, in charge of the juniors and seniors, whilst Miss Cox was in charge of the infants. They both had separate responsibilities for administrating their own school and teaching staff but were responsible to the Board of Governors.

They retired simultaneously in the mid-1940s and were replaced by Mr Joe Dixon and his wife Mrs Maud Dixon (infants). Mr Dixon brought a great love of classical music to the school, and passed on this delight to many of his pupils.

The school day always commenced with assembly in the large shared school hall. Senior and junior school first, followed by the infants.

As junior and seniors we fidgeted and coughed whilst sitting cross-legged on the wooden floor, surreptitiously whispering and nudging, flicking scraps of paper at our fellows, whilst we were sermonised to on all manner of religious matters from the Bible. Oh, how bored most of us were!

Eventually we stood to sing hymns. How we loved that after the tedium of the previous few minutes. We sang at the tops of our voices, while the piano teacher valiantly tried to keep up with us to restore some semblance of tune to the uproar.

The service always included a stern admonishment from the Head concerning our behaviour, threatening us to mend our ways, both in and out of school. We all shuffled guiltily, whether we had erred or not. His booming voice always felt like a personal reprimand to each child.

Beryl and I were always glad when this part of assembly had finished and we had not received yet another personal upbraiding. We were relieved that he could now turn his attention to the more major problems of the day.

These were usually to do with trespassing in the forest and the problems surrounding that particular breach of discipline, although it was sometimes for scrumping in Mendham's orchard.

A regular roasting was given to many of the senior boys because, during the war, tons of ammunition were stored by the military in Sherwood Forest and adjacent areas. Consequently our beloved haunts were put out of bounds to the general public.

Of course the older lads saw this as a challenge to their rights and so, using their local knowledge of the forest paths and ways, they spent many happy hours evading the poor guards on duty in order to purloin the dangerous goods.

"Boys from (either) Standard 7 or 8, out to the front!" the Head would bellow out during assembly at regular intervals.

The boys would shuffle forwards in their heavy boots, eyes downcast, heads bowed disconsolately for they knew what to expect.

"Empty your pockets," the Head rapped out.

Sure enough there was always ammunition to place carefully on the floor, along with all the other suspect debris that boys seem to accumulate around their person. Caning for the culpable youths always followed. However the stinging punishment never deterred the boys from sneaking into the ammunition shelters and pilfering the deadly playthings.

In later years, as the village has expanded and new buildings have appeared, many of the ammunition caches hidden by the boys have been discovered. In the 1980s, a small field at the side of the old school was raked and levelled by heavy equipment in readiness to construct a car park. The workmen were constantly taking their ammo finds into the Parish Council office.

To say they were disconcerted would not be putting too fine a point on the horrified concern they felt for their own personal safety. The forest itself has had to be cleared repeatedly by army bomb experts. The last time as recently as the 1990s. Although, in all fairness to my peers, the fault would not lie entirely with them. It has to be said that the military themselves must have been less than careful with the dangerous substances in their care.

I am pleased to report that my brother Ted was never one that was caned for this particular offence, but that doesn't mean he was actually innocent, perhaps just clever enough to conceal his hoard from prying eyes.

In their secret hideouts around the village, and in the forbidden forest tracts the boys would scoop the gunpowder from the cartridges stamping on the lethal material, smashing it between two stones and throwing all manner of things at the deadly stuff to try and get a blast, often achieving a satisfying explosion. How no one was injured remains a mystery. It is truly amazing that we managed to win the war, with what seemed to us to be such harmless material. The boys' lives must have been charmed, or Robin Hood was again taking care of his Merry Men.

After these dramatic scenes in assembly, we were all pleased that it was not us personally feeling the wrath of the Head. On command, we would all stand to recite the Lord's Prayer at breakneck speed, followed by a loud rendition of 'God Save The King'. Back to our classrooms we filed, the first ordeal of the day over. But sums awaited us!

Most of us tolerated school, but of course we had far more exciting things to do out in the fields and forest. However the law — but more importantly our parents — said we must be educated, so off we went. Reluctant heroes to do our duty.

I was never interested in sport of any kind, so I found the irksome task of throwing balls, leapfrogging, hurling bean bags to each other, running, jumping and various other athletic field pursuits a trial. I quite liked PE though, arm jerking, running on the spot, and turning in various directions. These I could tolerate. But most of my peers loved Games. The girls would play rounders or netball. The boys of course were either kicking a football about or playing cricket.

It never seemed to rain when we were children; the sun always shone on games afternoons, much to my chagrin. I would much rather have been cosily ensconced indoors with my beloved books. What a dreadful bore I must have seemed to my peers.

The girls were given lessons in housewifery, which included cookery classes and also taught various other aspects of housekeeping; how to iron shirts without a crease, a chore I detest and avoid to this day. How to dust and polish were more chores, I thought, than skills. I would try to evade them. Anyway who wants to learn how to polish silver? Certainly not me!

What I did enjoy was baking jam tarts, apple pie and a cheese and potato pie which fortunately my family seemed to relish, including Ted, who was not usually my greatest advocate. Of course it was sparse wartime rations at that time, so any extra food was always welcome.

Victoria sponges, apple dumplings and pies, the delicacies were never-ending. A great pity that we only did cookery once a week. I soon discovered that I wasn't much of a hand at beating butter and sugar together (too much like hard work), so would plead with my stronger-armed friend Winnie, who I remember with great affection, to perform this irksome task for me. I think I probably offered a peek at my sum book in exchange for this favour. The boys, meanwhile, hung around the cookery room door hoping the girls would pass them a spare jam bun, and we often did, after all they were our mates.

While we were doing wonderful things in the Domestic Science Room, which often involved pinching the dried fruit stored in the pantry (we were starved of these delicacies by wartime rationing), the boys were in the woodwork room honing their skills on lathes, drills and saws.

Ted brought home several lop-sided and wonky items that he had obviously sweated blood over. My mother greeted these offerings with rapturous acclaim, but they were soon consigned to an anonymous area of the house. Ted never seemed to mind.

I never considered lessons a chore, although I was not a particularly brilliant scholar, I think 'plodder' would have described me correctly. Reading, writing and arithmetic were second nature to me. History was a magical living experience. Geography took me to another wider world. I didn't greet sums with much enthusiasm though, a trait that has remained with me to this day.

I could never understand why all my peers were not as enraptured as I with the written word — but then again I couldn't catch a ball or run 100 yards at breakneck speed. I loved silent reading lessons. I was enthralled and was soon lost in the pages. One never to be forgotten afternoon, I received a slap on the cheek from the enraged teacher. It seems I had ignored her instructions to "put away your books, it's time for music now."

I was mortified, angry and insulted — engrossed in my fantasy world I had genuinely not heard her command. I rose from my desk and with great dignity stalked out of the classroom, marched home to my mam, who always put things right. Not this time however. Mam was far too much in awe of authority. "Back to school you go, my lady, and next time you do as you are told." No good pleading my case. Mam was adamant. Weeping and with my tail between my legs I crept back to school, and in fear and trembling entered the classroom.

"Come in and sit down. Are you over your temper now?"

I have often wondered since if that teacher was relieved to see me back, as she probably regretted her hasty action. I was never an easy child to deal with, even though I was a good pupil.

The one thing we dreaded was the regular visit from the 'nit' nurse. We were lined up class by class in the corridors and led into her searching hands and prying eyes. How we feared being told to, "Step over there and wait." That meant the whole school saw you in disgrace. As the line of children waiting to be inspected diminished the little bevy of children with lousy hair waited uncomfortably, knowing full well what they would be labelled by their peers.

It was a terrible experience, and I am pleased that neither Ted nor I ever joined the little band of disgraced children. The relief to be spared, yet again, was overwhelming. We skipped happily back to our classrooms. Even chanting Times Tables was better than being told to wait.

All the Infant rooms were set out in the same manner, the children sitting around four tables on small wooden chairs. The teacher's table was placed in front, which enabled her to overlook the whole room. Usually the teacher was to be found walking round the children giving them help and advice.

Colourful paintings and work was displayed on the walls, but though the atmosphere may have been relaxed very few of us moved into the Junior Dept. without grasping the rudiments of reading and sums. I loved being in the Infants, and for a short time I was given the very responsible job of Monitor in Miss Cox's room. I was proud as punch, even though it really meant that I was the dogsbody and dusted and tidied the room.

The Junior and Senior rooms were completely different from the Infants. They were arranged in four formal rows of double desks at which we were all supposed to sit in complete silence. Of course as with all children we could always be trusted completely. That is until the teacher left the room for some small task. We would explode into furious chat and high spirits until the return of the teacher. We would then fall over each other in the mad scramble to get our bums back into our desks.

"QUIET! Hands on heads!" would be the furious command. That was the worst torture in the world, as the blood drained away from our hands and arms and numbness set in. Even worse when you were commanded, "Hands down!" and the blood flowed back into your veins. Now that *did* hurt!

On the front wall of every classroom was a state-of-the-art rolling blackboard with cupboard space to hold maps and other teaching aids. Desk places were allocated by the teacher, which meant we were never paired with our particular friends. Perhaps just as well that Beryl and I were parted, it was certain that we would have caused ructions.

For much of my school life I sat with Keith. He had the patience of a saint, as I was a real fidget, constantly delving around in the depths of my part of the double desk. The desktop was not divided so when I wanted to investigate my goods and chattels I would give Keith a mighty nudge, which meant, "desk top up". He always obliged with never a grumble. Another of my foibles was that I was always convinced that people were copying my work, so I was permanently leaning over my desk, encircling my

Council School (c. 1935)

work with my arm. In actual fact they would not have gleaned a great deal if they had been peeking.

We had two favourite teachers; one Miss Woodhead, who became Mrs Bradbury, taught my class in her very first year of teaching and always declared that it was the best class she ever taught. Eventually she moved into the Junior school, and had the exalted post of Deputy Head for many years. We were lucky enough to be taught by her a second time.

Mrs Bradbury was a daughter of a long-established family in the village, who at one time kept the Jug and Glass pub, a confectionery shop and a wood-yard business.

Very rarely did the residents from the new part of the village venture into Mr Woodhead's shop; he was a very gruff man and intimidated us all. He did not make us feel at all welcome in his emporium. I understand that his bark was worse than his bite but I chose not to beard the lion in his den. So usually I chose to spend my penny for sweets at the 'New' shop, where what seemed like dozens of sweet jars were arranged on tempting display. What a decision. Should I have pear drops or gobstoppers or a small bar of Fry's chocolate? The penny was hot in my hand before the final choice was made and put into a screw of paper and solemnly passed to me by Mr or Mrs Milward, the tenants of the company shop.

Miss Fairfax, the other favourite teacher, was a daughter of the gardener at Edwinstowe House. They lived in a cottage in the grounds and Miss Fairfax was to be seen every school day pedalling sedately along Fourth Avenue, past the tennis courts and bowling greens, with her straight, autocratic back and every hair immaculately in place.

Life went along in the usual way at school, at home and in the village until war broke out, and it was all change for many years.

Pam Bird

L

LEMONADE

A photograph, taken around 1906, shows Mrs Robinson with her old pram on the Forest Corner selling Dandelion and Burdock, tea and Eiffel Tower lemonade to visitors.

LIBRARY

(**SEE ALSO:** PENNY LIBRARY)
There have been a number of libraries in the village. Christopher Thomson's library at the Jug and Glass appears to have been the first in the village. Before the pit was sunk in 1925, Mr Russon at the Post Office opened a library one night a week, with books displayed in wooden crates. Around 1939, the library was housed upstairs in the Physiotherapy Clinic, moving over the road to the Miners' Club in about 1942. The County Library Service provided a monthly book exchange. In 1951 a new library was opened by Fred Kitchen in the Institute on the High Street. The present library on the High Street was opened in 1971.

LOCK-UP

The former constable's cottage stands opposite the Jug and Glass. Chains can still be seen fixed to an outside wall. Prisoners were kept there overnight.

An Eighteenth-century Soldier from Edwinstowe

Sometime at the end of 1792, a letter was received in Edwinstowe by Mr John Cartwright. It had been posted in New York, America, in September 1792 by Samuel Bowring, Sergeant of Marines on board HMS Perseverance. The letter was addressed to his three sisters, Margaret Cartwright, Easter Tudsbury and Catherinah Bowering.

Samuel Bowring has just learned of the death of their mother and explains in the letter why it has taken so long for him to write:

"I have been taken prisoner by the French and lay in french prison almost eight months. They striple me of any clothing and every thing that I had and all my shipmates shared the saime faite. Ouer confinement proved verey harde and cruall. Blessed be my God I ham at liberty and restored to my elth and I ham in hopes that it will be in my power to have sume of theise nasti cruel papish French villanes in my care to rewarde them for theire usage to me."

As he had left a Will with his mother and his mother had died, this letter is to make a Will by which those three sisters were to act for him and receive anything of his. He is owed £50 wages from the ship Romiles, his present wages and prize money, the letter states.

Samuel probably received his education in the village school, which we know was in existence in 1719 when John Bullivant left money and land in his Will to pay the Master to teach eight boys. Samuel Bowring returned to Edwinstowe as a pensioner after the war. As was the custom of the time, he dropped down a rank. Corporal Samuel Bowring's name appears as a witness of some wills. There is no gravestone legible for him now.

Margaret Woodhead
(From a letter in Nottingham Archives)

MAJOR CINEMA

The cinema on Mansfield Road was built and owned by the Eastwoods. It opened in 1936. Newsreels were a great morale booster during the Second World War. Seats cost 3d, 6d and 9d to sit in the balcony. It was very popular in its heyday, but was recently demolished.

MAJOR OAK

In June 2002 the Major Oak was designated one of the 50 Great British Trees in honour of the Queen's Golden Jubilee. It may have been named after Major Hayman Rooke who catalogued the forest trees at the end of the 18th century.

Other names of the tree have included:

Cock Pen Tree – as fighting cocks were kept there.

Queen's Oak – a 19th century name, of obscure origin.

The Major Oak is still producing leaves and acorns although it is over 800 years old. It weighs 23 tons, and has a girth of 33 ft (10 metres), and a spread of 92 ft (28 metres).

MILLS

On Mill Lane there stood a windmill for grinding corn. There was also a water-driven fulling mill (for cleansing and thickening cloth by beating and washing).

The Field

I watch the field each day
Watch it changing with the seasons.
In winter it is bare; brown and barren
Or white with sparkling snow and freezing frost.
Spring follows, ploughing churns the waiting earth
And makes patterns straight and long.
The seeds are cast, then watered by the rain.
From bare earth small sprouting shoots begin to show.
Summer comes and the field is growing; green
Shoots struggle upwards searching for the sun,
Growing tall and strong,
Transforming green to glowing gold.
Autumn brings the harvest, the crop is cut,
Only sharp stubble remains, the field is shorn.
Then winter comes again, and earth is barren; brown.

Gill Empson

The Seed

Nature's magic trick, the seed.
A tiny speck, small as a grain of sand
Desiccated, dry, dull; it waits and waits
Sometimes for years, before it can transform
And become so much more.

A tall tree with leaves as broad as a hand
And roots which spread and feed the hungry plant
Or food to eat, mushroom, tomato, cool courgette,
Potato, beetroot, carrot, lettuce, astringent lemon,
Juicy peach, ripe cherry, crunchy apple,
Plums and apricots, dates and succulent figs,
Or aromatic herbs, rosemary, thyme and sage.
Basil, chives, fennel and sweet marjoram.

A beautiful flower with petals of crimson
Which open with the sun and catch the rain,
And send the scents to perfume the air,
Then fall and leave behind a legacy
Of many tiny seeds, scattered in the wind,
So nature's magic trick can be performed again.

Gill Empson

NEEDLEWORK — PARISH MAP

Inspired by Shirley Moore, local artist Peter Annable sketched local landmarks from photographs, which were then traced onto fabric (embroidery) or photocopied onto squared paper (cross-stitch). The map has a border of acorns and oak leaves. It took 40 people more than four years to complete. The cross-stitch Major Oak took over a year. Brownies made field boundaries with French knitting. The river is made of hundreds of glass beads. (Don't miss the King Edwin School girls' football team!)

The map was finally completed in 1996 and is much admired by visitors to St Mary's Church.

NOVELISTS

Geoffrey Palmer (born Rabbitt), born in Kirkstall Lodge. Published children's mystery stories in the mid-1960s, including *Greenwooders* and *Greenwooders' Triumph*.

(SEE ALSO: KITCHEN, FRED AND VILLA REAL FARM)

Joseph

The siren intruded into his deep sleep. He woke and wondered what had happened. There were no air raid shelters where he lived, the siren would be coming from Sheffield. Shortly after he was woken, there was a knock at the door. It was the air raid warden. "You need to report to the field next to Warsop Windmill," he said. "An unexploded bomb needs identifying, we've never seen anything like it before."

Joseph was the bomb reconnaissance officer for the area. He had been invalided out of the RAF with an ulcer, which made him feel guilty somehow, as though he had let his country down. This new job made him feel better; he was helping with the war effort again.

Joe was born near the beginning of the 20th century and was at school during the First World War. He wrote a letter to his Sunday School teacher, Sam, who had been called up to fight on the Somme. "How do you like being a soldier?" enquired Joe, with all the innocence of youth. He finished the letter with "From your scholar" and was very proud when he received a French picture postcard in reply.

As the oldest boy in the school, Joe was sent to the Post Office every day to bring news of the war. One memorable day he returned with the wonderful news that the First World War was over. Joe was very proud to have been given this important job.

As he travelled on his bike to the windmill, Joe felt excited about identifying the bomb. He could do something useful again and no longer feel a failure. Several members of the Home Guard were surrounding the bomb. There were potatoes everywhere, when the bomb fell it had uprooted them and scattered them all over. Anxious to examine the bomb, Joe had to wait till the field was cleared of all personnel. After studying the bomb in detail, Joe had to accept that he had never seen anything like it before and even though he consulted his manual, he could not identify what it was. His excitement abated and he began to feel useless again.

Officers arrived from Lincolnshire and Joe felt better when they too were baffled.

Eventually the bomb was identified, it was a 'pick-a-back', the first to be dropped in this country. The newly designed bomb sat on the back of a carrier which, when released from the plane, could fly some distance to a target. It was the precursor of the modern missile. No one was hurt by this bomb — it was a prototype and had not worked properly and the only injuries were to the potatoes. However, many more were dropped and did cause injury and loss of life.

Later in the war, Joe was called to investigate a German plane that had crash-landed at Warsop Vale. It ended up in the railway embankment. Joe had to search the plane to discover any unexploded bombs. When he arrived, there were two German airmen standing by the plane, completely unharmed but shaking with fear and shock. After inspecting the plane, Joe and some of the Home Guard escorted the airmen to Warsop Police Station and left them. There were no unexploded bombs, they had already been dropped.

Joseph had a long and happy life and died, aged 93, in Edwinstowe where he had lived for the last 13 years of his life. He had lost most of his sight and his hearing over his declining years and, near the end, a stroke took away his movement and his speech. However, he never lost his inner dignity, his sense of self or the grace and courtesy that had always characterised his relationships with others. He never put on anyone or did them down. The responsibility and service to others developed at his school during the First World War, in the RAF and as a bomb reconnaissance officer in the Second World War, stayed with him all his life. He was not an important man, except to his family, but everyone who knew him recognised him as a truly gentle man.

Gill Empson

OAKS

In 1695 the Duke of Newcastle promised Christopher Wren ten Sherwood Forest oak trees for the rebuilding of St Paul's Cathedral. There are 900 veteran oaks (more than 500 years old) in Sherwood, including the Parliament Oak (on Mansfield Road) where King John held a Parliament in 1212, and the Major Oak.

MANY FAMOUS OAKS HAVE BEEN LOST, INCLUDING:
Simon Fostor's Oak – used by a local man to shelter his pigs
Robin Hood's Larder (also known as Shambles Oak, Slaughter Tree) – the iron hooks inside were probably where a poacher or sheep-stealer hung his meat
Cuckoo (Birch) Oak – had a birch tree growing out of the top of the trunk

MODERN ATTEMPTS AT REPLANTING HAVE INCLUDED:
The TV naturalist, David Bellamy, who helped local schoolchildren in the mid-1980s to plant oaks in Sherwood Forest. Children nationwide raised money for the project.

There was also the Edwinstowe Oaks — Adopt a Tree Initiative
This was a joint project to help restore Sherwood Forest, undertaken by Austin Brady, Sherwood Forest Trust and local councillor, Pam Bird. Land was donated by Thoresby Estates. Sapling oaks and certificates were sold commem-

orating relatives and friends worldwide. *The Acorn Magazine* gave a donation to remember the children of Dunblane.

The wood was opened by Sir Andrew Buchanan, Lord Lieutenant of the County, in June 1999.

ODD FELLOWS

Birkland and Bilhagh Lodge was part of the Nottingham Ancient Imperial United Order of Odd Fellows. Christopher Thomson joined in 1833. He became so enthusiastic that he helped to open 40–50 other Lodges. He said that, "an anxious desire pervaded the congregated brethren, to better their social condition — to lay up sums of money, that by prudent forethought, they might be protected against the pangs of poverty, when disease or misfortune assailed them. They were also storing up ample funds to provide for the decent interment of any of their numbers, whenever death should overtake them. They were likewise studiously asking themselves how they could best provide for their widows and procure a home for their orphans."

He claimed that, "Odd Fellows' Societies have been eminently useful in convincing the working people of the advantages of union amongst themselves particularly so in the rural districts". In Edwinstowe hardly any members needed parish relief because they were self-reliant.

A request for land to build a hall was refused, on the basis that it would ruin village publicans if the Odd Fellows did not use meeting-rooms in local public houses.

(**SOURCE:** CHRISTOPHER THOMSON *AUTOBIOGRAPHY OF AN ARTISAN* J CHAPMAN 1847)

Edwinstowe Schooldays in the
1920s and 1930s

For me, schooldays in Edwinstowe began in April 1929. We had just moved from Moorends (Thorne Colliery village), South Yorkshire. Edwinstowe colliery village was still being built. King Edwin school was partly built and work was progressing on the rest of it. Our house was on West Lane and St Mary's church school was at the top of the lane, so that was the one I went to.

The three classrooms housed 150 children, rather overcrowded by today's standards. The classrooms were heated by a big pot-bellied stove in each room, burning coal or coke. Mr Greaves was headmaster, Mrs Greaves headmistress. He was also aided by Mr Land,

Mrs Pickard, Miss Draper (known to the children as 'Aggie') and latterly Miss Martin.

Discipline! Absolutely no fooling about then, the cane in each classroom hung in full view of all. Also for the senior boys Mr Greaves had a strap with one end cut to make three lashes (a tawse). When Mr Firth took over he threw it into the stove, watched in stunned amazement by all the boys in the room. He didn't throw the canes away though.

I remember one incident when I was in class one. A young girl, no more than five years old, was pulled from her desk by the teacher, down came her knickers, over the teacher's knee she went and was spanked unmercifully in front of the whole class. There are still a few people in the village who remember this incident.

The desk used by Mr Greaves was on a dais about a foot high. When Mr Firth took over he had the desk moved over the other side of the room. The dais was pulled down and underneath it scores of canes came to light, pushed there by the boys over the years through a crack in the woodwork, a forlorn attempt to avoid the forthcoming punishment.

Alongside the school was Manor Farm, now known as

Church Farm (I've no idea why Newark Council changed it). Three huge walnut trees dominated the stackyard. As the walnuts developed the lads would throw boulders and sticks up to knock down the nuts. There were two reasons for wanting the nuts: one, of course, was to eat them. The second reason was that walnuts grow in a husk and the juice in the husk stained the fingers brown. The juice liberally rubbed on the hands and fingers, it was claimed, contained an ingredient that took the sting away should you be caned. It never worked for me.

On one occasion ten boys were throwing things up at the tree nearest to the school. I was one of them. A boulder went through a skylight on the school roof, breaking the glass. Mr Greaves lined up all ten of us and informed us that the cost of replacing the glass would be 5 shillings (25p today). So each of us would have to take sixpence to school the next day, or we would be caned. This was about 1931 or 2 and times were hard — sixpences were hard to come by. I was eight or nine years old at the time and in company with other nine mates, all lined up the next morning for the cane. Nobody took sixpence.

With the farm being alongside the school we became familiar with the various jobs to be done as the seasons altered. In October Mr Herbert, the farmer, would come to school to recruit potato pickers to gather the crop and to remind them to bring their own buckets. The school had a week's holiday for potato picking.

As we grew older, other tasks gave us the chance to earn a few pennies. At harvest time there were no state-of-the-art combine harvesters then. All the work was done by horses. Pulling the binder round the field to cut the rye, barley, oats or wheat, we would follow behind, stooking the sheaves to dry out. When dry, the sheaves would be carted to the farm stackyard to await the arrival of the threshing set. The big steam engine would pull the threshing drum into the yard and work would begin. By now the stacks were infested with mice and at playtime and dinnertime the boys, armed with thatch pegs, would be killing

80

the mice. There were heaps of them. The whistle would go to go back into school and the boys, as usual, would pick up half a dozen dead mice each and throw them at the girls as they lined up to go into school.

Considering there were 150 pupils in such a small school the education we received was very good. No doubt the strict discipline at the time certainly concentrated the mind.

Across the road from the school, where the Major Cinema later stood, were the school gardens. All the boys were taught how to work a garden. Two boys to each plot. At that time almost all the boys upon leaving school were employed on local farms and the gardens of the big estates, Thoresby, Rufford, Clumber and Welbeck. With the coming of the Thoresby Colliery it all changed and the vast majority of school leavers went to the pit. So did I, when my time came, aged 14.

Until the arrival of Mr Firth, sporting facilities did not exist at the church school. Mr Greaves showed no interest in football or cricket. Not even a sports day. Mr Firth soon had a football pitch set up, helped by Thoresby estate who made the goal posts. It was on Mr Herbert's grass field where he kept his cows and horses — cowpats liberally spread across the field. It was 'interesting' when the football landed in a fresh one, as it often did.

I believe it was the 24th of May that a ritual took place at school. It was Oak Apple Day. When you went to school in the morning you had to have in your hand a bunch of new oak leaves. In the other hand you carried a bunch of nettles, carefully wrapped round the stems with a piece of cloth to prevent them stinging you. If any unfortunate child failed to show the oak leaves they were stung on the knees and legs by the others. This was the time of short trousers for the boys and some of their knees were painful to look at. Thankfully the custom died out. Apparently it originated when Charles II was compelled to hide in an oak tree to escape his pursuers.

In the early thirties there was very little money about.

The pits were only working two or three days a week as there was no demand for coal due to the world recession.

After we came out of school at 4 pm many of the lads would go to the local farms to work in the fields. I used to go to Mr Naish at Forest Farm in spring time, crawling along the rows of swedes, mangolds or sugar beet singling out the plants. By knock-off time we had earned a few pence and a pair of sore knees and fingers. At harvest time we would pitch the sheaves onto the cart to take them to the stackyard. This was the best time. Mr Naish would send one of the men to the Royal Oak pub across the road with two milk cans for the beer. We all got some. A pint for the men and a half for the lads.

Jim Houghton was one of my classmates; he lived in one of the cottages next to the school. His father worked for Mr Herbert. After school was over (4pm) in springtime, Jim, armed with a big clapper, would be tramping across the newly sown cornfields rattling away to scare off the rooks and crows that were thought to be eating the seed corn. It was called 'crow tenting'.

Around about 1931 the Bolsover Colliery Company, who owned Thoresby pit, decided to start the pit trip. All the wives and children would be taken to Skegness for the day. The men had to pay if they went. It took four trains to get us all there — Edwinstowe was deserted.

Until the pit trip began I had never seen the sea. Very few of my friends had seen it. We had heard how wonderful it was from the children whose fathers worked on the railway. Now we were going there too. There were three big annual events that we looked forward to: birthdays, Christmas and, now, the pit trip.

Aged about eleven it was time to go to woodwork classes. No facilities existed in Edwinstowe schools at that time so we had to go every Friday to Whinney Lane School at Ollerton. We caught the Ebor bus to Ollerton and Wass's bus back home. The fare was 2d each way. Parents paid the 4d and were reimbursed by the education committee every three months. Mr Foot was the woodwork teacher —

Church School 1930/31
(Joseph Bennett is at the end of the row on the right)

he was a good one too. If he caught you using the tools the wrong way, a swift crack across the knuckles with a piece of dowel would quickly rectify things.

In summer, if the weather was good, most of the boys would run back to Edwinstowe so that the 2d bus fare was ours to spend. We walked everywhere; nobody owned a car.

The playground at church school stood alongside Mansfield Road surrounded by iron, spiked railings to separate the boys from the girls. There were no indoor toilets then, the toilets were outside. Even at King Edwin, a new school, all the toilets were in the yard outside.

Hard times — but mostly happy ones.

Joseph Bennett

P

PENNY LIBRARY

Despite having a large family, Christopher Thomson (formerly a strolling player/scene painter) was so keen to buy the *Penny Magazine* that he gave up having sugar in his tea.

In 1836 Thomson and friends tried to establish an Artisans' Library and Mutual Improvement Society, but potential members "thought that to pay down *five shillings for books* was the very height of extravagence, if not of madness!"

On 1st January 1838 he started the Edwinstowe Artisans' Library — subscription one penny per week. It was an instant success. He soon had 50 members and a library of books at the Jug and Glass public house. The Earl of Scarborough became their patron.

During the winter evening classes were held to teach arithmetic, literacy and debating. A passionate advocate of self-education, Christopher Thomson said, "Ignorance is living death".

(**SOURCE:** CHRISTOPHER THOMSON *AUTOBIOGRAPHY OF AN ARTISAN* J CHAPMAN 1847)

PHYSIOTHERAPY CLINIC

As a result of proposals by the Thoresby Colliery Underground Sick Club Committee, this unique facility was opened in 1939 at 110–112 Fourth Avenue. For a small weekly contribution its services were available to miners from Thoresby and Clipstone, their wives and children. Sister Beeley and her successor, Miss Holland, each serving as physiotherapist for 25 years, dealt with up to 2000 visits per month. Every three weeks a top orthopaedic surgeon held a surgery at the clinic. In 1997 the clinic became a registered charity and is now staffed by physiotherapists from Chesterfield. Treatment is available to the public on payment of a fee per visit. (Contact: 01623 822374)

POST OFFICES

Edwinstowe's first post office stood on the High Street, on the site of the library.

1851 – Stonemason and Postmaster William Cottam. Nearest money office Ollerton. Grocer and sub-distributor of stamps Richard Marston.

1895 – Letters were brought from Ollerton at 7.30 am. Evening collection left at 4.40 pm weekdays only. Money Order Office and Savings Bank.
(**SOURCE:** *KELLY'S DIRECTORY*)

1930s – Purpose-built next to Bullivants (Forest Lodge on Church Street). The Post Office insignia is still visible over the door. Later moved to Mansfield Road (now Bright Beginnings Nursery)

1990s – Moved to Mills Newsagents on the High Street.

Outlaws

The village
devoid of Lincoln green
where never leather met with willow,
sinks slowly
into post tourmatic shock,
the summer syndrome closing
into winter hibernation.

Now only the sleeping policemen sing
as raw anger flies down the high street
in a blaze of burning arrows.

Linking past, with present,
myth, with reality,
hope, with self destruction.

Writ large in yellow graffiti
on oak.

Sue Allen

H. Symonds Grocery Shop and Post Office, High Street c1912.

QUERCUS PETRAEA

The durmast or sessile oak — it has long-stalked leaves and stalkless acorns.

QUERCUS ROBUR

Latin name for the English or pedunculate oaks, like the Major Oak. It has stalkless leaves and long-stalked acorns.

Ricardo

My name is Richard Nardini. *Ricardo*. Perhaps the name
Nardini seems familiar? There was that Scottish (*Italian!*)
actress in — oh, what was the name of that programme?
Or if you've travelled to the West of Scotland you might
have come across the Nardini ice-cream empire. You'll not
get a wafer like them. Cousins, they are. Well, distant
cousins. All the Nardinis are related.

And that's where you start if you mention the word
Italian. Ice cream, followed quickly by opera. And to that
older generation from the war there might be mention of
cowardice. I'll come back to that later. No, I'll come back
to that now. Listen, I met a man — a British soldier —
whose squad had crashed through the front line as it
moved north in Italy and became stranded behind the
German lines for months. People risked their lives to look
after those soldiers and he joined the partisans, doing
damage. He didn't use the word cowardice. It's just that
for a lot of my father's generation who were in the Italian
army, it was not their war. They were not fanatics. They
could see what Mussolini had dragged us into. We didn't
hate the British and we didn't hate the Jews either, lots of
our soldiers hid Jews. Disobeyed orders. Look it up.

But listen to me. "Us" this, "we" that. I was born in
Nottinghamshire. My dad was Italian, like a few around
the village he stayed on after the war, after the POW
camp. Truth is, there was too much poverty to go back to
then. There was work here, and quite a few local girls were
attracted to somebody just that bit different. My dad
talked about how they would laugh at him and his mates
as they stumbled over their new language. But there was
never any scorn. People felt sorry for them, miles from
home, missing their families. So that was that then.
Anyway, my dad had fallen out with his immediate family
before he left. He was a Communist and in Edwinstowe
he'd fallen in with some others, pitmen mostly. Over in

Mansfield they had some big meetings he said. Not as big as back home but it was enough.

Working on his own though and with a new family he'd drifted away from the Party. The *Daily Worker* still came every day, but I don't think he read it. On the wall in the front room though was a photograph he'd framed. It was only a reproduction torn from a magazine, but it looked good. Some Spanish artist had painted a picture of a man conducting a socialist choir. It was a big choir, and the workers had red kerchiefs round their neck and looked so proud. I don't know what they were singing but seeing that every day made me want to sing. And that's how I ended up in Mansfield Operatic Society. This time it was my dad's turn to laugh as I struggled to pronounce the Italian words. He started to teach me the language. Mind you, it was the dialect from Turin so a lot of the words did not quite tally with the operatic words. Still, I was the nearest to an Italian speaker the Opera had. I suspect a linguist would have been a little surprised to find Mansfield Opera Society singing with this broad, working-class Turinese pronunciation. My dad's family had been small farmers and he'd finally come into the city when it expanded and got involved in the Party. He built cars and was just getting established as a carpenter in the film industry when he had to become a soldier. It meant my mum's food shelves stayed up though, and he was never short of work here, fixing things.

It was a long time after the war before he got back in touch. His parents had died, a couple of the family — Benita and Alfredo had stayed around. Benita never married and lived in the family farm, rented out the land, or sold bits off every now and again when she was short. Alfredo married a girl from the next door farm, Melena, and moved in there when her parents died, so he at least kept up the family tradition.

I used to visit when I was in my teens. The old family feuds were no longer that relevant. Foreign travel was in its infancy for most British people but a lot of the Italians travelled to and fro. Working there when the economy was good, working here when the economy was bad. Quite a few were in the cafe trade from pre-war days — I have relatives all over Wales! I spent a couple of summers helping out on my uncle's farm and kept in touch after dad died, the same year as mum.

I never married. Yes, there were a few women in the Opera over the years who I'd sung a few duets with, on and off the stage, but never the right one for me.

So next week I'm off. Edwinstowe's changing and my house is worth a lot now. I'm off to Turin for good. I'll stay with Benita outside the city until I can get my own place, or maybe I might just stay on. She's finding it hard to cope on her own and it would be nice to grow stuff on the land she's kept back.

Richard Nardini

ROBIN HOOD WAY

Inaugurated in 1985 by the Rambling Club, supported by Nottinghamshire County Council and the Countryside Commission. The footpath is a 105-mile walk through Robin Hood country that starts at Castle Gate House in Nottingham and finishes at the steps of St Mary's Church in Edwinstowe.

RUSSIAN LOG CABIN

Exhibited in London, purchased in 1874 by the Duke of Portland and erected as a hunting lodge in the forest near Warsop Windmill. No nails were used in its construction. Although the cabin was very picturesque, it fell into disrepair and was demolished in 1954.

My Garden of Gifts

Sitting in my garden chair
I thank God for every gift
Every flower, all so fair
Like candytuft and thrift

Anemones and forget-me-not
Clematis on the wall
Roses, I have quite a lot
And sunflowers so tall

But it's not just the flowers
Whose joys will never cease
It's also that I can spend hours
In contentment and in peace

Every springtime I give praise
For my garden's great rebirth
Sure that in countless ways
A garden's heaven here on earth

Bill Currie

All the Fun of the Fair

I'm longing to go once again
To a good old-fashioned fair
Today they have white-knuckle rides
But they really don't compare

We also had a roller coaster
And the big wheel too
But we also had the tunnel of love
Which we could sail right through

Down a board we'd roll our pennies
And many a dart we'd toss
Strolling around the fairground
We'd eat our candyfloss

Climbing upon the merry-go-round
We would be taken around and round
Then we'd slide down the helter skelter
Until we reached the ground

Past the boxing booth to the ghost train
Which scared us half to death
Then we'd ride on the Waltzer
Until we were out of breath

After a ride upon the dodgems
Down the cakewalk we would go
We would try to walk along it
As it jerked us to and fro

We'd maybe have some supper
A hot dog or meat pie
And many a coconut has been won
On the good old coconut shy

White-knuckle rides may be thrilling
But when all is said and done
I'd rather have a travelling fair
Which definitely was more fun

Bill Currie

S

SPIDERS

There are more than 200 species of spider (and more than 1,500 species of beetle) in Sherwood Forest, including the rare wolf spider, which has nasty habits!

SSSI

2004 celebrated the jubilee of the Birklands part of Sherwood Forest being declared a Site of Special Scientific Interest. In 2002, in honour of the Queen's Jubilee, it was also made a National Nature Reserve (NNR) and is a candidate Special Area of Conservation (cSAC) under the European Union's Habitat Directive.

STATION

Edwinstowe station has four platforms. It was opened in 1896 by the Lancashire, Derbyshire & East Coast Railway company and marketed for the tourist trade as the Dukeries Line. The Dukeries Hotel (now Ma Hubbard's) with its large dining room was built in 1897 by Mansfield Brewery anticipating an influx of visitors. The station was officially closed to passenger traffic in 1956, but summer specials to Skegness ran on Saturdays until September 1964 and goods traffic until 4th January 1965.

Growing up in a Mining Village in the 1930s and 1940s

4. The approach of war

As in the rest of Great Britain, war did not come raging into Edwinstowe like a wild tiger. Its oncoming was slow, insidious and frightening. Fear on heavy foot stalked everywhere. Rumours flew around the meeting places in the village. The shops were full of housewives carrying on with their usual chores and shopping, but sharing with each other their mutual concerns and fears about the future of their menfolk and the welfare of their children.

Many of them had already experienced the ravages and terrible consequences of the Great War. They were devastated to think that the world was once again about to be plunged into bitter conflict. They knew from painful experience that war was not a romantic dash by valiant men rallying around the flag, to save their country. It was a bloody and continuing nightmare to be endured, amidst tears and manifold hardships. They also recalled that despite the great victory in 1918, the miners, along with many other returning heroes, had been treated shamefully, and were thrown on one side to fend for themselves as best they could.

The men sitting in the pubs, drinking pints of foaming beer after their wearisome shifts down the pits, fought the War again in words. Peace had descended upon this country just a scant 20 years before. They too feared for their families and their new way of life. They were weary of confrontation and battle both at home and fighting for their country. They had come a long way in the last decade whilst fighting their own formidable struggle with politicians for the right to a decent livelihood.

Those that had served in the First World War had firmly believed when they lay down their arms for the final time in 1918 that they had fought a war to end all wars. They were again faced with the spectre of muddy and rat-ridden trenches, lice, partings from loved ones, death, crippling and disabling wounds. Even the hard and filthy work down the mines was better in comparison.

As children we heard chitchat amongst our parents about the bleak outlook, but at this point it did not really affect us. We were still fed and clothed, and we could still go out to play, and school was still open five days a week. The threat of war first affected our family in a very strange way. One weekend in 1938, before war was declared, my mam and I travelled by two buses to visit her sister Elsie, who lived in Clowne. This was always a wonderful treat, both for my mam and I. Mam and her sister were able to catch up on family gossip, whilst I played happily with the local children, whom I had got to know very well.

I loved my Auntie. Like my mam she was kind and loving and nothing was ever too much trouble for her. Ted and I often took it in turns to stay for the weekends in her lovely grey stone cottage. We were thoroughly spoilt on these occasions, and made to feel very special. These were our only relations living close enough to visit on a regular basis, so the extra love and attention was very welcome. On this particular weekend we arrived as usual, but instead of just Auntie and Uncle and cousin Stella greeting us, there was a newcomer waiting to greet us.

Hannah was a little Jewish girl who had been whisked away from the persecution of the Jews in Germany. She had travelled on one of the Kindertransports, which had been organised by well-wishers to evacuate the children from certain death at the hands of the Nazis, who now held Germany in thrall. Herr and Frau Ramer had seen their tiny daughter board the train with other children at Gelsenkirchen. They bid her a tearful goodbye and were never to see her again. What heartbreak that must have been for all the parents, knowing only too well their own future. The ghettos awaited them, and the hell camps of destruction. Their fate was sealed, but they had managed to send their beloved children to England and safety. Hannah was four years old.

My aunty and uncle became Hannah's new foster parents. She could not have been made more welcome by anyone. Although they were not wealthy in money and possessions as her parents had obviously been, they were able to give her a home rich in loving care and laughter. What more does a child need?

I looked over this little stranger very carefully. She was so different. I had never previously seen a foreign child. In fact it was doubtful that I had ever met a child that did not come from a mining family. Her skin was clear and olive coloured, her face framed by tossing, short, black, glossy curls. Her dress was of green shot velvet, her stockings were white and lacy, tied at the knee with bouncing tassels. On her feet she wore gleaming black patent buttoned shoes. On her wrist she wore a flashing gold bracelet, and the tips of her fingernails were gleaming white. She was a vision.

I had never seen such expensive clothing before, or heard such funny language. Hannah could not speak a word of English, but she chatted away as though we could understand every word. At first I was very puzzled, but the international language of all children is play, and so it was not long before we began to make ourselves understood whilst playing Cats Cradle.

Hannah continued to live with the Finches for many years, soon becoming part of the family. Because of the circumstances surrounding her, she was brought up as a little English child of a working class home. Unfortunately she soon forgot her mother tongue and also her Jewish religion. There was no one in Clowne to teach her of her heritage, although my aunty and uncle did chat to her of her family roots. Unfortunately they knew very little of her background to impart to her.

At the end of the war, a miracle happened for Hannah. Her uncle and cousin Max had escaped the Holocaust and had come to England seeking their only other living relative. What a wonderful reunion! Every weekend Hannah was taken by her uncle to stay with him and to worship at the synagogue in Sheffield. She was taught to read Hebrew. After some tuition themselves, my aunt and uncle helped her to keep all the Jewish festivals and ensured that her food was prepared in the traditional manner. Hannah Ranier had regained her heritage.

This was wonderful, but heartbreak followed for my aunt and uncle. Her ties with her only living relatives had strengthened. Hannah at the age of fifteen went happily to live with her uncle and cousin in Sheffield. Not very far away from her foster parents, but still parted from them. Despite their sorrow, they knew this was the way forward for their darling child. Their long and loving work had come to an end. Hannah later married a Rabbi and went to live in Israel.

One day in early 1939, a very important looking gentleman appeared at our door. He was wearing a suit and carried a briefcase, which was an unknown accoutrement to our family in that day and age. He had come to register the family for National Identity Cards. After much painstaking writing and searching questions, we were each presented with a blue and white card.

"You must carry this at all times, it is a very important document," warned the official to all the family.

During the period that this interview was taking place I was transfixed, sitting on the sofa in the kitchen swinging my feet, listening avidly to this gentleman, and thinking how exciting all this was. Now I was being presented with my very own Identity Card complete with number. People did not usually give us anything. Of course I did not realise the significance of the document at the time. I remember that number to this very day. Much later those numbers given to everyone were transferred to the Medical Cards required to register for the newly formed National Health Service.

Things were now moving apace. Our next visitors brought and fitted us all with gas masks. They were horrid and smelled disgusting. We looked like pigs with black faces. Mother declared that she would never wear hers, she would rather die first, it was so claustrophobic.

Now, that was enough for me! I would certainly not wear mine if my mam was going to die. Eventually I calmed down, but I never forgot those few throwaway words of my mother. They always haunted me. Could I be sure that mam would put the dreaded thing on if there really was a gas attack? In the event there was never cause to wear it, but *would* she have done so if necessary?

The masks were all issued complete with a square cardboard box and a string with which to sling it around your person. Mother decided that the safest place for the Identity Card was in the Gas Mask box. So into the boxes went the cards, where they remained for the duration. We took this important box with us everywhere slung around our persons. It was like an extra appendage, we ran, skipped, jumped, ate our meals, went to the lav; we lived our lives with this cumbersome box bumping around. In class we hung them on the back of our desks, but did not move without them.

Woe betide anyone who arrived at school minus this box. It was a capital crime — even worse than pinching ammunition. Mam never allowed Ted and I to forget ours, and despite her earlier protestations, mam carried hers all over as well.

Eventually some entrepreneur of the day decided to make Gas Mask Box covers. Some children sported leather look covers, whilst others had the cheaper canvas version. However, some poor souls still carried their naked cardboard boxes, and they were often barracked about this. I was very relieved that Ted and I at least had canvas covers.

One day there was a very sinister happening at school. A huge closed van arrived on the school field. We were all agog! What was this all about? We were soon to find out.

Each class was taken to the van, instructed to don their gas masks and then ushered into the van. It was quite scary and dim inside and gradually the atmosphere became thick and a hazy yellow. Even Beryl and I were scaredy-cats on this occasion. We clung to each other's hands in fear.

"Are you frightened?" I whispered.

"'Course not," came the quavery reply.

But I knew she was, because I was. We were having our gas masks tested! When we came down the steps onto the field, we were all so relieved, but with great bravado we assured each other that it was nothing. Of course, big man Ted and all his friends told us of their adventure and managed to embroider some gory details around the experience. They swore they had not been a bit frightened, but we knew better. We did not believe them! Fortunately all was well, but I have often wondered what would have happened if there had been a faulty mask, or an hysterical child to deal with. I am pleased to say the van never returned to the school.

However the next stage to the gas mask saga, was yet another important person turned up. He issued all of us with a fitment which was screwed on to the gas mask. Things were getting worse by the day. We now resembled black pigs with emerald green snouts!

Many of the children attended Sunday School at one or other of the two Methodist Chapels in the village. Just a few children attended the Church Kindergarten which was held in the Church Rooms. (After 3rd September 1939 the name was quickly changed to Sunday School.) These services were regular events in our lives. We were scrubbed, dressed in our Sunday best, with shoes gleaming, and off we went. I never heard a child complaining about this Sunday ritual. Our elders and betters thought we should go for religious instruction and who were we to argue. I spent many hours looking at the drab walls in the Chapel, just existing until the Lord's Prayer was said and we were released.

101

Ted and his friend Lewis always went for a walk afterwards, and I was dragged along, little fat legs running behind trying to keep up with these two young lords. They walked for miles, and I would be utterly worn out. No dallying though. They might just go without me, and leave me in the middle of a lonely field on the way to Ollerton. Or lose me in the bogs which they assured me were underfoot. These two lads had instilled into me that I must always tread in their lengthy footsteps to ensure my safety. I would stumble along petrified in case the bog monster swallowed me up. I was very young and gullible. Even today I pass that particular piece of land with beating heart.

One Sunday, after one of these lengthy marathons, we arrived home hoping the delicious aroma of dinner would be awaiting us. Not so. Instead mam was sitting on the sofa in 'The Room' crying, and dad was standing with his back to the fire looking very stern. My first thought was, "I'm in trouble for some misdemeanour that I've committed, but just which one?" Ted was also creasing his brow. Was he thinking the same as I?

Dad then told us, in a very serious voice, that whilst we had been at Sunday School Mr Chamberlain had been on the wireless and war had been declared. Was that all? We two children were relieved. We thought whatever 'war' was it didn't really affect us. How very wrong we were. Ted was just twelve and I was eight.

Pam Bird

T

TELEPHONE EXCHANGE

From 1907 to 1910 only the public houses and a few farmers had telephones. "Even the village sergeant didn't have one. When the station wanted to get in touch with him, they phoned the landlady of the Jug and Glass public house and she had to run and fetch him. She had to do this during the Great War when there was an air raid." *(Recalled in 1986 by the landlady's daughter, Edith Cole).*

With the advent of the colliery, an exchange was built onto the post office on the High Street and a lady telephonist from London arrived to take charge.

THORESBY COLLIERY

It was originally proposed to call it Edwinstowe Colliery. The adjacent large, handsome mansion, Cockglode House, was demolished in the 1960s. It was the first all-electric, fully-mechanised colliery. It was also the first pit in the country to produce 1 million tons of coal per annum in 1951. In 1925 there were two shafts 690 metres deep. In the 1950s they were deepened by 109 metres.

THORESBY HALL

Built between 1864 and 1875 to Anthony Salvin's design, it was the former home of the Manvers family. The television adaptation of *Great Expectations* with Charlotte Rampling as Miss Haversham was filmed there, before the house was sold to Warner Holidays who spent £14 million converting it into a hotel. Theatrical performances and art exhibitions are now staged in the stable block throughout the year.

The Courage of Love

It stole across the horizon to slowly and silently wait

It hung like a mist in the distance, without form or shadow or
shape

Like an unwelcome lover, intent upon stalking its prey

Deceptively hiding its presence in the actions of each busy day

Each night it continued its journey, ruthlessly seeking its goal

Until it knew it was able to reach out and swallow you whole

Its intangible mantle approached, casting shadows the heart
would deplore

Stealing the light from your life force, and sickening your soul
in its core.

Like a fog it clings to your airways, impeding each breath that
you take

It traps you into a nightmare, from which you cannot awake.

Some will call it an illness and say it's a sickness of mind,

Some will call it indulgence, of a selfish and self-centred kind.

Some come with their cures and quick fixes, some turn on their
heels and run;

Some may sit down right beside you, and promise the return of
the sun.

But the soul that is sick from depression is devoid of all hope,
and can't share

In the promise of brighter tomorrows, or the love of someone to
care

The soul that is sick with depression has moved to a far distant
plain

Where hope is abandoned and lonely, crushed in a turmoil of
pain

To a world where sunlight can't enter, and love can seem lost
in the dark

Despair is Lord of this region, so barren, and lifeless and stark.

A soul that is sick with depression can't reach out and walk to
the light

It feels lonely, rejected, abandoned. And lost in the dead of this
night.

A soul that is sick with depression, lives in a world where the
   vampires abound
To feed till the soul that's so sickened, is unable to utter a sound
They thrive as they feed from your life force and drain it of all
   it can hold
Till weak from the loss of its life source, the soul withers, and
   starts to grow cold
Only the love of true friendship can survive in this terrible place
To carry the hope of salvation, and lead the soul back to its
   rightful and God given Space.

Sheila Norton

UNDERGROUND MAN

Nicknamed "the Burrowing Duke" and "the Mole-Duke", Lord William John Cavendish-Scott-Bentinck, the eccentric 5th Duke of Portland, resident at Welbeck Abbey, employed upwards of 1500 men to construct three underground libraries, a chapel (later the ballroom) and a network of illuminated tunnels wide enough to drive a horse-driven coach through. He was rumoured to spend £100,000 per annum on building projects.

(**SOURCE:** MICK JACKSON *THE UNDERGROUND MAN,* PICADOR 1997. SHORTLISTED FOR THE BOOKER PRIZE)

Cobham Brewer's Labour of Love

If you had visited Edwinstowe vicarage in the 1890s you might have encountered a bald-headed gentleman with a long, grey beard and large, grey-blue eyes pottering in the garden. As Reverend Dr Ebenezer Cobham Brewer told a reporter, gardening was his only vice.

In his mid-eighties, he was busy revising his famous *Dictionary of Phrase and Fable* — checking 1,300 pages at the rate of 48 double-column proofs a week. The *Dictionary* was first published in the 1870s and it had already sold 100,000 copies despite the initial reluctance of the publisher, Mr Cassell, who thought it was a "doubtful speculation, quite beyond the wildest reach of the imagination" and urged Brewer not to make it too learned nor include too many Latin quotations.

True to his recipe for a long life: "Little to eat, less to drink, little sleep and plenty to do", having worked until 3 or 4 o'clock in the morning, he was still down to breakfast every morning at 9.00am sharp.

He spent time each evening with his grandchildren, "telling stories, showing the treasures he had collected in various countries and relating his experiences at the court of Napoleon III".

He was a welcome visitor at the village school where he helped the boys with their mapping skills and awarded an annual prize. Although he'd never had a parish, he often assisted his son-in-law, Reverend Henry Telford Hayman, preaching sermons and conducting weddings. He also took a lively interest in the restoration work on St Mary's Church, which was completed just after his death in March 1897.

Born at Norwich in May 1810, Brewer was by his own admission, "very backward and idle as a boy". His three brothers made successful careers — John Sherren, a University Professor; Robert, a Baptist Minister and William, a doctor and MP for Colchester.

Ebenezer studied Law at Trinity Hall, Cambridge, supporting himself by his writing. Probably hoping for a college fellowship, he was ordained in 1838. However, when he left university he taught at his father's school, succeeding him as headmaster.

In an age of self-help, his educational books were instant best-sellers. The first, *A Guide to Science*, in question-and-answer form was translated into many languages and sold half a million copies. He prepared a French version for the Prince Imperial, using examples from French life. Another 40 books followed, covering everything from miracles to single-entry book-keeping.

In the 1850s he joined Cassells, which published books in affordable parts for poor people who wanted to improve themselves, such as *The Popular Educator* at 1 penny a week. When the children's series, *My First Book of...* was launched, Brewer wrote all twelve books.

In 1856 he married a clergyman's daughter, Ellen Mary. After her death in 1878 he moved in with his eldest daughter, Nellie, at Ruddington Vicarage. His grandson Perceval Hayman, recalled his grandfather's bed-sitting-room wall "covered in plain white paper upon which he used to write in pencil stray memoranda and the names of any particularly interesting visitors and the dates on which they came to see him".

Dr Brewer moved with the family to Edwinstowe in 1884. When the beautiful Duchess of Portland visited the Vicarage she insisted on going upstairs and carrying on a long conversation with Dr Brewer sitting on his bed, "a highly informal proceeding in those days, which particularly pleased the old gentleman!"

He told a reporter from *The Westminster Budget*, "My method is very simple. I always read with paper and pencil at my side and jot down whatever I think may be useful to me and these jottings I keep sorted in different lockers. This has been a lifelong habit with me and compiling them into a volume consists chiefly in the selecting, sorting, explaining, correcting and bringing down to date. My literary references are all contained in these pigeonholes behind me, each letter having its own bundle of slips in their turn all running in alphabetical order. This system of commonplacing I have kept up regularly for nearly seventy years, and the fruits of it are embodied in my various books. In fact, the Phrase and Fable dictionary and the other books of that class may be said to be merely different sections of one gigantic commonplace book. The labour of all this writing out and indexing has been very great,

Dr E. Cobham Brewer (seated) with his family outside Edwinstowe Vicarage (c. 1899).
Left to right: *Reverend Henry T. Hayman, grandsons Charles and Perceval, his daughter Ellen Maria with Phylllis.*
(PHOTOGRAPH: EDWINSTOWE HISTORICAL SOCVIETY)

though a labour of love for me. I calculated once that in my time I must have covered manuscript enough to fill this room from floor to ceiling..."

Brewer died on 6th March 1897. The *Evening Post* reported, "by the time fixed for the ceremony a large number of the residents of Edwinstowe had assembled in the churchyard to pay a last tribute of respect. The mourners included the Countess Manvers. The coffin was covered in beautiful wreaths and choice exotics. The undertaker, Mr Herbert Woodhead, was paid £6/10s for the oak coffin, £1 for 4 bearers and £1 for 6 pairs of gloves".

Brewer's grave is marked with a cross and is under a beech tree a few yards from the west face of the tower. His name lives on not only in updated versions of *Phrase and Fable*, but also in such improbable publications as *Brewer's Cinema*.

Liz Stewart-Smith

VICARAGES

The site of the earliest vicarage is unknown. The second (home of E. Cobham Brewer), on Church Street next to Edwinstowe Hall, was demolished. The third (the boyhood home of Cecil Day Lewis) was a large Victorian vicarage set back from Mansfield Road. The fourth was exchanged with the village doctor for Ashgrove House (a Queen Anne house) on West Lane. When Ashgrove House was demolished, the present vicarage was built on the site in 1973.

VILLA REAL FARM (Mansfield Road)

Joseph da Costa, a Jewish merchant, arrived in London from Lisbon in 1726. His daughter, Kitty, married a rich old man, Joseph Villareal. When he died his widow became involved in a famous breach of promise case. She then married William Mellish of Blyth and converted to Christianity. Her children, Sarah and Abraham, were christened Elizabeth and William. Elizabeth (Sarah) became the first person of Jewish origin to marry into the peerage when she married Viscount Galway.

Her brother, William (Abraham), bought a farm at Edwinstowe and married a Mansfield girl, Elizabeth Halifax. He had ambitions to be an MP but died at the age of 30. He was a well-liked local benefactor, according to the memorial plaque in Edwinstowe church.

His widow, Elizabeth, was well provided for, but made a very foolish marriage to Mr Gooch, who stole her fortune and denied her access to their two young children. She ended up in the Fleet Prison for debt. Her *Appeal to the Public* (1788) and *Life* (1792) attempt to counter her husband's slanders and put her side of the story. She later went on stage with a strolling theatre company. Under the name Elizabeth Sarah Villareal Gooch she published several novels and a book of poetry.

(**SOURCE:** GERTRUDE & M.J. LANDA *KITTY VILLAREAL* JEWISH HISTORICAL SOCIETY, PURNELL & SONS 1936)

The Tree

Majestic oak
Spreading magic over the forest
Ancient oak
Existing for hundreds of years
Living oak
Bursting into life each spring
Dying oak
Hollow with scents of death and decay
People's oak
Thousands wonder at your magnificence
Nature's oak
Huge yet created from a tiny acorn
Robin's oak
So many legends, so many secrets
Amazing oak
Needing support but still growing
Major oak
The jewel in Sherwood's crown

Gill Empson

The Forest

Ancient trees, living history
What secrets do your branches hold?
Oak and ash and silver birches
When will all your tales be told?
Ancient trees, living forest
Where is your inheritance?
Fern and yew and maroon beeches
Have we almost lost the chance?
Ancient trees, living history
Why are your mysteries unrevealed?
Hazel, holly, hawthorn hedges
Your secrets are forever sealed.

Gill Empson

WAXWORKS

In February 1887 Mrs Jarley's famous waxworks visited the village, providing a source of amusement. The scenes represented were "You dirty boy", "An Italian Organ Grinder and his Monkey", "Sairy Gamp administering Mrs Winslow's Soothing Syrup", "Plough Boy eating a turnip", "Mr Dotheboys's flogging Mobbs into a happier state of mind" and "The Execution of Mary Queen of Scots".

(**SOURCE:** *1887 CHURCH MAGAZINE*)

WEATHERCOCK

There is a weathercock on the spire of St Mary's Church. A bullet from a German aircraft put a hole in it. When the spire was repaired, local schoolchildren jumped over the weathercock — before it was replaced on top of the tower!

WELLS

Deep wells have been discovered near the Black Swan, the Royal Oak and Manor Farm. They have been filled in for safety. Piped water came to the village in 1905.

Severn Trent still extract water in the Sherwood Pines area because it is not contaminated with chemicals.

WINDOWS

The hidden face of a young woman, showing her mouth, nose and eye, in the East Window of St Mary's church could be the donor, Miss Cutts, or the "signature" of the maker, Henry Hughes. The Archangel window in the Lady Chapel is in memory of a local benefactor, Captain Alexander, who lived at Edwinstowe Hall, but died in Bermuda. He was a distant cousin of William Alexander, Bishop of Derry, whose wife Cecil Frances was a prolific writer of children's hymns (*There is a Green Hill, Once in Royal David's City* and *All Things Bright and Beautiful*).

WINGS FOR VICTORY

During the week of 19–26 June 1943, there was a week of activities to raise £20,000 to buy Mosquito aircraft. Donors stuck special stamps onto a bomb, which was displayed in the Major Cinema foyer. Whist drives and dances were held in the Welfare Hall. On Saturday night the Army Cadet Bugle Band, accompanied by tanks, paraded through the village to the Forest Cricket Ground.

Prince of Thieves

"Is he here yet? Sound the horn again. He must be on his way by now."

The group huddled closer together inside the enormous trunk of the big oak tree. The cold clammy night engulfed them in its blanket of mist and the earthy smell of the undergrowth was overpowering. It was a sorry sight to witness. One of them, a portly fellow dressed in the drab garb of a monk and nicknamed Friar Tuck because of his indefatigable appetite for food, preferably of the greasy variety, apparent from the large stains down the front of his chest, was becoming increasingly agitated. As, also, was a skinny red-clad figure with sad, blood-shot eyes who went by the name of Will Scarlet. He moved closer to Friar, gaining warmth from his ever-perspiring body, retching slightly as he accustomed himself to the foul smell.

"Blast the man," the Friar bellowed, startling the remainder of the party. "He's two hours late already. Dawn will be with us soon and the trip will be in vain."

Little John, the tallest of the group, stamped his feet impatiently as the waiting continued. "Come on Robin. It's been two days since my last trip," he muttered to himself. He patted his pocket nervously to check the cash was still there. The old lady who had contributed to this fund had been easy pickings. The dear old thing had been pushing her trolley happily along the High Street, evidently happy to be out in the fresh air when she had stumbled and fallen off the uneven kerb. John had been the first on the scene with a helping hand and consoling charm. "Whoops! That's a nasty graze you've made there on your knee, and just look at your tights. Come on, hold onto my arm and show me where you live. I'll have you home safe and sound in no time." She linked her arm in his and beamed at passers-by as she enjoyed being escorted by such a handsome fellow. They were soon entering her quaint little cottage. Delighted to have company, she busied herself making a cup of tea. John eyed the room with glee. In the corner was a beautiful mahogany cabinet displaying a variety of valuable ornaments. Seizing the opportunity he hastily pocketed the carelessly abandoned jewellery from the dish on the sideboard together with a selection of the smaller ornaments. Only a fleeting wistfulness had passed through his mind as he compared the old lady with his own grandmother. Having enjoyed her hospitality he was soon on his way to contacts eager to relieve him of his wares.

Will, a small figure, dark-haired, with a haunted but still impish face, dressed in his shabby red anorak, had been obliged to work harder to obtain his cash. Sitting on a cold pavement, playing his flute pitifully all day long, gathering the meagre coins offered by passers-by certainly wasn't easy. Still, he had accumulated enough to make his purchase. His thin emaciated body looked in need of some wholesome food but it was the last thing on his mind. Gone was the time of his university life when his study of music had filled his every hour.

The hooting of the night owl broke the eerie silence and the rustling of the undergrowth as the forest's night creatures scurried along in the quest for survival. A sudden movement and rustling in the tree startled the group and they scrambled to their feet in preparation for the invader.

Jester Jed swung down from the spreading branches landing in the middle of the group, and tried to uplift the dreary crew with tales of his nightly jaunts when he smashed his way into parked vehicles stealing their contents and sometimes the cars themselves. Then he would drive around with wealthier areas breaking into houses, garages and garden sheds. He considered his quest for cash much more exciting than some of his mates.

"We need some heat around here. Come on Beth, help me light a fire," he called to his devoted female follower. He hastily gathered twigs and bracken until he had a suitable heap and then with a sprinkle of petrol he set it alight. The flames flickered over their desperate faces and the crackle of burning twigs drowned the sound of their despondent chatter. Beth, in her dream-like state, marvelled at Jed's ability to bring cheer to the watchful group. She had forsaken her home of luxury and comfort; her devoted parents and promising future, to seek refuge with these her soulmates. Her hair, once golden and silk-like, now hung lank and lifeless around her ashen face. Her brown eyes, which once sparkled and teased, were dark pools in its midst.

"Hear that?" cried Will, alert now as he recognised the hoot of a horn in the distance. A mad scramble for a prime position to view the approaching figure unfolded. Excitement heightened as they clambered up into the trees, pushing and shoving. Cheerful banter ensued as they peered out into the gloomy distance. At last out of the semi-darkness strode their saviour, dressed from head to toe in gleaming leather gear, followed close behind by his shadow — the strikingly beautiful Marian — her leather suit clinging to her shapely figure. Eagerly they sprang down from their perches and clambered forward to greet their desirable visitors.

"Out of my way vagabonds. Give me space." Robin commanded as he and Marian took ownership of the entrance to the tree. "Who's chasing the dragon tonight?"

They hastened towards him, cash at the ready, and eagerly took possession of the small pouches of white powder. Their eyes now bright with anticipation they took on a more cheerful persona and ripples of laughter and giggles rose from their midst. They each scurried off to their makeshift beds of boxes, old rugs and blankets, comfortable now in the knowledge that they could return to their dream-like state of existence in their weird world of hopelessness.

"Here, Friar! Take this bag of food and see they get a decent meal." Robin tossed the sack over.

"Most charitable of you my Lord," Friar Tuck retorted as he ambled forward to catch the proffered gift.

119

Delivery completed Robin and his maid made their royal exit.

"Farewell, my Merry Men." He was out of view within seconds and the distant roar of his motorcycle went unnoticed by the group now hell-bent on seeking oblivion.

The sound of the retreating motorcycle was suddenly overtaken by a cacophony of sound — police sirens, screeching brakes, slamming doors. The undergrowth crackled as approaching feet tramped through the disturbed night. The sniffing and barking of dogs grew nearer as did the beams of torchlight.

"Sergeant! Over here," the shout went up as the officer approached the befuddled group. He rubbed his hands in silent satisfaction as he contemplated catching Robin in his net.

The not so Merry Men stumbled forward forlornly unaware that their true saviour had arrived in a new disguise.

Enid Johnson

X FILES

The former fashion shop on the corner of East Lane was believed to be haunted by the ghost of a seven-year old girl who drowned playing by the river, when she fell and hit her head. She was said to break light bulbs and one Christmas, when the shop was closed, threw clothes and handbags around the room. After that the owners took care to say goodbye to her whenever they locked up the shop.

The best-documented ghost is at Ollerton Hall. It is believed to be the ghost of Colonel Thomas Markham, a Royalist officer who was killed at the beginning of the Civil War before he could enjoy his elegant, newly-built home. In the 1900s several local people had violent encounters with this phantom including the Edwinstowe constable who was attacked when he attempted to arrest the ghost close to the site of Thoresby Pit.

Early one winter evening in the 1980s, several local witnesses observed a UFO. It hovered silently over Rufford School for several minutes before flying off towards the forest.

Haunted Rufford

November. The day is dying early, and beneath the trees it is almost dark. I park my car down by the main road and get out, and lock it, leaving it there. The shrill beep of the immobiliser echoes from the trees. The evening is quiet. The sound of cars on the main road faint already, screened by the undergrowth and trees.

The abbey isn't visible from the road. A winding avenue leads down to it, so overgrown with trees that, though it is barely late afternoon, it is already dark beneath them. I pause a moment and look back towards the car, thinking that it would be best to return in the morning. Rufford is beautiful on a crisp autumn morning. But I'm here to see the ghosts and what better time than a late November twilight? I press on, buttoning my jacket up to my neck and shoving my hands deep into my pockets, trying to calm the sudden, sharp increase in the beats of my heart.

The abbey was founded by the Cistercian monks of Rievaulx Abbey in the twelfth century. Isolated in the depths of the forest of Sherwood, their neighbours must have been, more often than not, the bandits and outlaws who found sanctuary in the dark glades and overgrown wilderness. The monks were hardy men, accustomed to asceticism and self-sufficiency. It is perhaps, then, unsurprising that some of those souls are thought to linger still.

Walking down the avenue of lime trees, shedding their leaves rapidly now as the year expires, I imagine the dark cowls of the Cistercian monks, hoods pulled down, shading their faces so that they seem but ghostly shadows sliding quietly between the black silhouettes of the trees.

The Cistercian abbey is half ruined now, the windows gaping holes through which bats turn. The brickwork is grey and forbidding in the half-light. In the window of the Tudor mansion a pale light glimmers and I stop and gaze up towards it.

The abbey is said to be haunted by one of the Cistercian friars. The ghostly monk wears a black habit. He stands immensely tall, his fleshless skull palely visible in the shadow of his hooded habit. Most that have reported seeing him have caught a glimpse of him in the gilded mirrors of the hall, flickering in the darkness behind their back. Or felt the soft tap of his bony finger on their shoulder, so that, turning, they are confronted suddenly with his empty sockets, the deadly grin of his long exposed teeth, the hollow, dark depths of his skull. The face of the grave. A sight that stopped the heart of one Edwinstowe man in the early 1900s. He was found face twisted in a rictus of terror, waxily white in the light of the candles of those who rushed to hear what had caused the dreadful howl.

Or so I imagine, stood in the gathering gloom, on the path before the old house. The Black Friar's victim is buried in a nearby graveyard. In the parish register it reads that he 'died after seeing the Rufford ghost.' Above my head the bats wheel darkly. The gathering night is still. Silent. The crackle of dead leaves startles me, and I turn and scan the undergrowth, the shadows beneath the trees, too deep to be penetrated by the wan light of the rising moon. I see nothing. Perhaps it was no more than a hedgehog rooting in the darkness. Logic tells me so. Tells me that it could not have been the shuffling, skeletal feet of the Black Friar. I know that. Still, I feel a cold shiver run down my spine.

The Black Friar, though, is not the only apparition that haunts this old abbey. As I walk around the hall, I take care to make a wide berth of the buildings, avoiding the blackness of the shadows beneath the broken abbey walls.

The Savile family came into ownership of the hall in the seventeenth century and the place was frequented by kings and nobility. Some female guests' stay was, though, disturbed. Many women told of how they woke in the cold watch of the night to find a presence in the bed beside them. A cold, clammy baby that nestled up close; a pathetic child finding terror where it sought comfort.

And there are more. A woman dressed in black has been seen by many, flitting noiselessly through the trees, weeping. I glance across towards the hedges, and the narrow lanes that cut out into the woods and know that I should walk there, that if I am to research these apparitions seriously I should venture away from the safety of the open lawn. But I don't. Even the thought of the animal cemetery makes me shiver; remembering childhood visits, hanging over rusted railings, deciphering the names of pets once loved, long dead.

After the dissolution of the monasteries Rufford fell into the hands of Bess of Hardwick's husband and became the haunt of royal parties, up in the region for hunting. The weeping woman is said to be the ghost of Arbella Stuart. Her young parents, Elizabeth, the daughter of Bess and Charles Stuart, were married secretly in the chapel at Rufford. Elizabeth I, and King James who followed, were suspicious of Arbella, fruit of this union, born and christened in Rufford; she was a more direct heir to the throne than James, and there were those in the country who wanted to see her monarch. She is known by some as the Lost Queen of England.

A passionate, woman, she fell in love with William Seymour, who also held claim to the throne. The marriage was expressly forbidden by the king and when it was discovered that they had been wed, they were both imprisoned. In 1611 she affected a daring escape, dressed in the clothes of a man. She had arranged to meet her husband at the coast where they would take a boat and flee to France, but when it drew late and he had not arrived, she was urged to fly anyway. The weather blew up a storm on the channel, keeping Seymour from meeting her *en route*. Arbella was captured and imprisoned in the Tower of London.

Of her last few years Disraeli wrote, 'What passed in that dreadful imprisonment, cannot perhaps be recovered for authentic history — but enough is known; that her mind grew impaired, that she finally lost her reason, and, if the duration of her imprisonment was short, that it was only terminated by her death.'

And so she wanders still the quiet grounds of Rufford, where she was conceived, mourning the loss of her love. Her grief was imagined in a poem by Felicia Hemans:

'Farewell! — the passion of long years I pour
Into that word: thou hear'st not, — but the woe
And fervour of its tones may one day flow
To thy heart's holy place; there let them dwell —
We shall o'ersweep the grave to meet — Farewell!'

Will, one night, their unquiet souls meet upon the lawn of Rufford? Or in the deep shade of these nocturnal woods — their love having o'erswept the grave? Perhaps that is one ghost I wish well, I think, turning back to the sweeping drive, making my way carefully, ears pricked, heart still thumping, to my car.

Stephan Collishaw

YOUTH HOSTEL

Opened in May 1998 on the site of the former Coal Board Laboratories, facing the cricket ground. It uses the latest environmentally friendly, green technology — an underground sump stores rainwater for flushing toilets, the roof is insulated with recycled newspapers. There are micro-switched windows and computer-controlled heating thermostats. Funding for the project was gained from the single regeneration budget and EU Regional Development Fund. It cost £650,000 and sleeps 45. (Contact: 01623 825794)

Growing up in a Mining Millage in the 1930s and 1940s

5. Entertaining Times

In the mid 1930s, Edwinstowe, like many other British villages, was just learning about the 'pictures'. The cinema was a wonderful medium that was gradually infiltrating from towns and cities to the rural parts of England. The entrepreneurs of the day saw an opportunity to cash in on the lure of the amazing magic screen. New picture palaces were springing up in the mining villages around, but none so palatial as our very own Major cinema.

The opening of this magnificent edifice in 1936, opened up a new world of glamour, romance and exotic locations not dreamt of in the prosaic world of the miner and his family. The magic screen transformed the mundane, everyday life of our small farming and mining community. We were accustomed to washed-out Walpamur decorating our walls, rough coco-matting on the red tiled floors and horsehair furniture. In contrast here was luxury in abundance — red plush seats, wall-to-wall carpeting, the sumptuous Art Deco interior with fairytale lighting, two sweeping and majestic staircases, polished wood — everything richly embellished with gleaming brass fittings. And all this before we even saw a film. How posh Edwinstowe had become.

We all loved to go to 'the pictures', which were screened twice nightly, changing programmes thrice weekly. Young and old were seen flocking every night (except Sundays — that came later) towards Mansfield Road for their Hollywood 'fix'. We children had our own wonderful 'tupenny rush' on Saturdays. We were enthralled. There was little bad behaviour; we were all too engrossed in the magical world unfolding before us. We staggered out into the bright light of day, excited and longing for the next instalment; the outcome of the inevitable cliffhanger. We had left Tarzan being attacked, or our favourite cowboy about to be shot by Red Indians or, horror of horrors, our heroine tied to a railway line by her wicked suitor.

Adults (accompanied by children, if we were lucky) watched Nelson Eddy and Jeanette MacDonald serenade each other in *Rose Marie*. The ladies discreetly wiped their eyes at Clark Gable and Vivien Leigh as their romance waned and died in *Gone with the Wind*. Laurence Olivier, Bette Davis and others became our screen idols. Technicolor was an amazing revelation. We in our tiny village had never realised that the sea was so blue, the grass so green, or that coconuts grew in wonderful palm trees surrounded by grass-skirted maidens dancing on the beach.

Then came World War II and the residents were joined at different times by British troops from nearby camps. American soldiers, German and Italian Prisoners of War, Displaced Persons from Eastern European countries. The queues of people waiting to get into the Major, stretched four deep to the gates of the Cenotaph. They endured the lengthy vigils without complaint; chatting about world events, or flirting whilst awaiting their turn.

The Major was now the focus of village entertainment, plus of course the beloved 'Saturday Night Whist Drive' and 'Dance at the Welfare Hall'. We roared with laughter at the antics of Abbott and Costello, roamed the range with Gene Autry, Hopalong Cassidy and others of similar ilk.

News of world events was brought to the riveted audience by the Gaumont British Newsreel. We watched with disbelief and sorrow when our men were to be seen fighting a bloody war in foreign fields. Hollywood brought us the world of make-believe, *South Pacific*, *Annie Get Your Gun*, *Seven Brides for Seven Brothers*, *The Wizard of Oz*, *The King and I*. The list was endless. Everyone knew the music from these shows; the melodies were hummed and whistled all round the village.

We marvelled at the dancing of Fred Astaire and Ginger Rogers, we romanticised with Judy Garland, sang with

Mario Lanza, Doris Day and Frank Sinatra. The girls swooned over Rock Hudson and Gary Cooper.

During all these passing years the Major was presided over by manager, Mr. Len Blythe, an extraordinary gentlemen, always immaculately attired in black suit and bow tie. He ruled young and old alike with a rod of iron. Any fooling about and you were out. However, one look and one thrust of his mighty chin was enough to quell the most outrageous behaviour. His usherettes, all girls from the village, were smartly attired in gold and green uniforms of which they were very proud. Shall we ever forget the Eldorado ice creams, dispensed in the interval by these young ladies? Sheer mouthwatering delight after a wartime diet.

Now the Major is no more, demolished in the wake of TV and computers — solitary entertainment — leaving a poorer Edwinstowe and the passing of a great era.

Pam Bird

Z

ZEROS (2000)

The Millennium was celebrated by a procession lit by homemade lanterns and ending in a service at St Mary's Church. In the summer, a pageant written by local people was performed in the forest accompanied by the Thoresby Colliery Band.

ZEST

A Victorian song about the Vicar and other Edwinstowe characters was "sung with zest" at village gatherings around 1900.

Joe Woodhead's Song

Muster Hayman the vicar
He sings a good song;
And preaches a good sermon
That's not very long.
T'owd Mitchell the Sexton
He tolls the big bell;
Tommy Thomson plays organ,
Joe Woodhead blows well.
Chorus:
Oh this Edinster, wonderful Edinster
Edinster, ba gum, is a wonderful town!